Playing House

the paradox of paradise

Volume III

Also by Joseph D. Reich

If I Told You To Jump Off The Brooklyn Bridge
(Flutter Press, 2009)

A Different Sort of Distance
(Skive Magazine Press, 2010)

Pain Diary: Working Methadone & The Life & Times
Of The Man Sawed In Half (Brick Road Poetry Press, 2010)

Drugstore Sushi (Thunderclap Press, 2010)

The Derivation Of Cowboys & Indians (Fomite Press, 2012)

The Housing Market: a comfortable place to jump off
the end of the world (Fomite Press, 2013)

The Hole That Runs Through Utopia (Fomite Press, 2014)

Taking The Fifth And Running With It: a psychological
guide for the hard of hearing and blind (Broadstone Books,
2015)

The Hospitality Business (Valeviel Press, 2015)

Connecting The Dots To Shangrila: A Postmodern Cultural
Hx Of America (Fomite Press, 2016)

A Case Study Of Werewolves (Fomite Press, 2018)

The Rituals Of Mummification (Sagging Meniscus Press,
2017)

Magritte's Missing Murals: Insomniac Episodes
(Sagging Meniscus Press, 2017)

How To Order Chinese During A Hostage Crisis: Dialects, Existential Essays, A Play, And Other Poems (Hog Press, 2017)

American Existentialism (Tuba Press, 2017)

An Eccentric Urban Guide To Surviving (Analog Submission Press, 2017)

The American Book Of The Dead (Xi Draconis Books, 2018)

From Premonition To Prophecy (Delinkwent Scholar Press, 2018)

Statutes Of David (Pen & Anvil Press, 2018)

I know why old men sit in front of windows all day sighing & crying & living & dying when the sun goes down on the city at night (Kung-Fu Treachery Press, 2020)

Makeshift Press
114 Wild Rose Circle
Winchester, VA 22602

© 2020 by Joseph D. Reich

All rights reserved. This book or parts thereof may not be reproduced in any form, stored in any retrieval system, or transmitted in any form by any means—electronic, mechanical, photocopy, recording, or otherwise—without prior written permission of the publisher, except as provided by United States of America copyright law. For permission requests, write to the publisher.

Cover art © 2019 by P. Forester
"Love or Confusion" is printed here with permission of P. Forester.

ISBN: 978-1-7341558-2-2

July 2020
MakeshiftPress.org

PLAYING HOUSE

"One velvet morning when I'm straight
I'm gonna open up your gate"

- Nancy Sinatra

Prelude:

If history has a tendency to repeat itself can't we
just get it right once? It's simple and obvious to blame
the mad scientist but how about the blind masses of blissful
ignoramus' who voted him in? Satire invented for a reason…

1.

everything you see in those old *poloroid* snapshots
pretty much sums it all up for our time on earth all
within that thin white frame with smudged pastel
colors seeping together; the strange smiles and
very proud poses, poised, poignant on lapping
seashores right below dilapidated boardwalks
of lost insane funhouses; all those taboo secrets
which we just got used to and learned to accept
(became our reality without conflict or question)
in the blissful madness of split-level suburbia; the
human pyramid of tumbling children from the dead
end, racing those faded, red *radioflyers* like mad all
the way to the end of the world where we were destined
to just fall off in our flannel and cords happily ever after
while in the moment just didn't really care or give a damn as
was all about adrenalin and passion so why'd any that matter?

proof a,

at the end of the dead end
where wild woods stood
you likened to the end
of the world where
you'd fall over
so stayed far
away from
which was
a fear of the unknown
and the nature of folklore
and sort of felt strangely
enough something safe and
secure and stable about that

proof b,

those days when neighbors
were more neighborly
and everyone knew
everyone else and
just show up to
screen doors of
back porches and
ask moms if they had
any *fudgetown* cookies
as they'd just say something
like "hold on for a minute honey"
and shuffle towards their pantry

proof c,

kids being brought
out on stretchers
in superman outfits

proof d,

when that first amphibian crawled out
of the ocean for purposes of pure instinct
or curiosity in the initial stage of evolution
who could have possibly imagined that whole
string of sparkling towering condominiums
in honolulu overlooking the pacific and gilead
the muscleman with his early morning stretches
surrounded by milf goddesses pretty much
ironically involved in the exact same range of
motions; anyone know a good nightclub or sushi?

2.

memory foam
an ingenious idea
for going back to
where it all began

like the foam from the sea
on the remains of the beach

3.

                i remember i used to
                      work at this place
                            called *soho books*
      on west broadway
             in new york city
                    & whenever
we'd get in our
      weekly delivery
              & have to unload
all those big boxes
      of books
            one of my favorites
was about how
      to build a dinosaur
            out of chicken bones
while now when
      i look back at it all
            that's alot
    of what i just think
          life is
            wondering
                    where it all went wrong
            & the source to all those
    things you lost somewhere
            down the road
                trying to reconstruct
& put it all back
      together
            with chicken bones

proof:

language can never fully express the conflict of the tortured soul
you can lay low in the drizzle speaking to your freudian and at
best return home like buddha with the world off your shoulders

knowing there was no real world to begin with
in the first place just the stray scent of pungent
fermenting magnolia and women lying topless

tormented desperate on the mediterannean
looking to be rescued by some savior-
son-season they once believed in

instead he's satisfied with a fresh slice of mozzarella
and shrimp straight out the shell on a bed of linguine
in his wrinkled flannel suit writing haiku to the gods

while just follows the foreign wives with a buzz
at sundown into some pharmacy under the palms
knowing not what to say but exactly what he wants

4.

thinking about those times with those girls
you had fallen in love with had fallen out of love
the confusion and conflict with all those maddening
dramatic ones on those long slow train rides crawling back
and forth from the city to the suburbs dwelling and brooding
about it all made love or the concept of what you thought
love was supposed to be during that strange lovely period
interlude and surreal life-transition very much worth living

5.

a whole to-do list
of things and directions
you were allowed to do
and not do to them (and
became like some control
model/poster child due to
past suffering and losses)
for their own personal
fantasy of experimenting

6.

the best thing about them
is after you do the act or deed
in a beautiful fit of frenzy in one
natural graceful awkward motion
how they pull their clothes back on
again self-conscious self-effacing
with modesty like angels come
to life at the scene of a crime
and become like that neighbor
you always dreamed of and
now like some sacred sleazy
member of the family make
life worthy and worth living

7.

women make
houses for the living
guys for the dying
both versions of
living happily
ever after

8.

i never much cared for those jokes
"a guy walks into a bar" i guess cause
i never very much cared about the crowd
in there nor for that matter what happened
to them and most of all the straight man...

proof:

just think of that one happy hour! happy hour!
happy hour! happy hour! while always just
seems like some of the biggest assholes
and losers who haven't been laid forever
or no one who loves them or at jobs they
can't stand (yeah i know we all suffer from
some of the same symptoms) as all in their
own personal psychological prisons (soon
to become loud or silent drunks) trying for
just this one last-ditch desperate moment to
accomplish contentment as they just get more
obnoxious and boisterous, and can see why
wouldn't want to spend a single second with
them and have to invent certain kinds of thematic
sayings like happy hour (5-7) to drag them all in

proof:

you see an ad on your tv for a special
on boneless chicken wings and think
how can that even be? is that like some
fallen angel during like some final call at
happy hour with his/her head in their beer
mug staggering home drunk all alone from
karaoke night during the change of season?

9.

things always seemed the best
                & most meaningful
                              when i had very little
    like coiled
        in the fetal position
            by some spitting
                steaming radiator
whether it was
    a futon on the floor
        in the lower east side
                & brooklyn
or that soothing, hypnotic one
            beneath midnight
                    frosted lattices
    of my girl's tick-tock
        toasty foghorn kitchen
                    pensive, naked
            in sleepy hollow
    those coughing, choking
            pipes
              which
        warmed up
    my fiance & i's
autumnal bourbon bedroom
        pumpkin floorboards
            in the frozen inn
    of algonquin, maine
                            looking out over
            the whole massive, insane sea
    calming all neurotic
    nihilistic fears
& anxieties
        in my late-teens taking long
                sentimental cat naps
                        with my head
                    down deep
              leaned up against
        it like some stirring conch shell
    hearing it lyrically
        kick on & off

                              in rhythmic
                                        synchronized spirit
                                   ruminating
                         during winter break
               from college
enraptured with dylan's
                    "nashville skyline"
                              having fallen madly in love
                                                  for the first time
             with a gorgeous german girl
                         with blonde hair
                              & big blue eyes
                                        (be still my beating heart!)
          when all was still & silent
                         strolling solitary
                              becoming one
                                   with winter
wonderland forest
          from brooding backyards
                         to secret brooks
                                        trickling through
                                   pachysandra
                    to sweet succulent
               swirling chimneys
                              to gazing
                    into each other's eyes
          encompassing all of life
                         in the late-night
                                        flickering
               candlelight
                         of taverns
tucked into
     twinkling snow
               piled-up high
                         outside
          the crystal prism
of magical windows
                    when finally at last
                         there was blissfully
                                   nowhere else to go
          somewhere on the outskirts of town
                    flowing between your whole

broken-boned boyhood
& holy here & now

proof:

looking back at love
what love used to be
was her whispering
in the early morning
in sing-songy voice
"joey are you up?"
already having
packed luggage
with coffee ready
as if climbing up
the side of masada
at dawn heading
towards your next
european city and
town always through
the window of some
rushing train having
already seen most
of southern spain
when all you got left
is cordoba and grenada
as if heading to the first
and last palm tree at
the end of the world

10.

your grandfather clock and grand piano creep
delicately past your door like a mischievous boy.
apparently they have a charity function to attend.
the ice fishermen are heading to the lake with their
three stooges equipment and bottles of wine & whiskey.
that pretty girl in her maroon velvet dress doing figure
eights beneath the bleak beautiful mountain. holy
sacred swizzlestick smokestacks from the paper
mill milling over misty swollen rivers where the
whole red brick town is wrapped in blankets having
absolutely no need to go out from the frosty lattices
of the season at last protected within fantasy dreams
escaping and getting away from all that lurks beneath

11.

that part of the season when the rivers return again
with their purple-blue ribbons rushing radiant beating
through the branches not having yet blossomed new
leaves moving miraculously weaving in and out of
the village and back out up into the mountains where
mother nature in flannel and faded blue jeans with
long flowing chestnut hair has given birth to a whole
beautiful brood of brilliant rambunctious filthy monsters
with wild enthusiastic accents and her ramshackle tumble
down shack leaning up against the back of the traintracks
where tomboys and delinquents full of mad spirit try
on their seduction and all great new adventures begin

proof:

young stud soldiers literally sweet-talking
pretty blushing high school girls in cobblestone
alleys somewhere between chinese and the pharmacy

the day ends with grilled cheese & bacon
in boxcar diners beneath the mountain…

12.

just a little more courage and a little less superstition
to get by in this motherfucker— always slept so well
in rundown motel night before taking on those rapids

ex: most superstitions, defense-mechanisms
(the development of coping and survival skills)
or the fear of loss of a possible beloved guardian
or authority figure come in the form of some
transitional-object like a teddy bear or security
blanket, only to one day hopefully be substituted
by certain socialization skills with integration into
one's psychosocial environment, to find much later
on in life (whether ironic or not) in one's later stages
of growth and development to be afflicted with the exact
selfsame, high-expressed emotions, empty and vacant state
of being, existential angst, and one's brooding mortality to
eventually be replaced by one's own free will and volition
or self-determination toward mature, intellectual relationships
or some other form of positive and productive, creative sublimation

Proof: a place they can never take

1

Just off the Tappan Zee...
on the day of our breezy blue wedding
a Cosa-Nostra walks his dog and bids me
good morning. He makes a nice living and
I return his greeting as the eager Autumnal
boughs bend back to see what's happening.
Children's science experiments glisten
through trees. The violins begin and
I dig in. The series tied between San
Francisco and The Angels. Our band leader
announces the first dance and me and my
blushing bride sneak into a room of clapping.
I swear I heard too a bit of booing, but that's
neither here nor there. Toasts are thrown and
they have to restrain me. Relatives who have
grown much gloomier, grizzlier over the ages
having not gotten closure over formally-held
grudges creep across the dance floor like
Neanderthals with jowls dropped to their
ankles and blossoming bifocals that somehow
appear upside down. They pass down punchlines
about the burdens of marriage and I mechanically
nod my head up and down and release myself from
their hands. I think they think this is what makes
us men. They appear lost and sad. From what my friends
said eagles circled overhead. To me this was the perfect
image of a blissful type of dread, as they smiled and
scowled, the living and the dead. I feel guilty that I
didn't speak more to my favorite cousin from Wisconsin.
She looks pretty and lonely and holy as always. I talk
to my best friends outside the old sunken shipwrecked
inn. They are well-groomed and handsome, shy and smoldering.
My wife and I's cabin smells exactly like camp when I suppose
we were supposed to be happy; in times of Sanford & Son and
The Doobies. She sweeps rose petals and Hershey's Kisses off
the sheets and we finish the night off with a carafe of milk and
carrot cake; unlatch the door to usher in the breeze and whatever

smells may still be lingering. I love my girl because she's funny
and snappy and will kick the crap out of me whenever she finds
it necessary. I feel most comfortable with the rabbi because he is
is short and sweet and simply says he has to leave early to transport
the teen witness back to Jersey. No promises are made with napkins
and matchbooks and getting together in the future. We will be making
a donation to some Israeli foundation when we return home from
Athens. The day after, upon further inspection my sister tells me
the whole affair seemed rather romantic and that it brought about
a certain amount of good feeling. I suppose that's the best that
can be expected. The next day I see my sad and striking bride
beneath a throw. She says cold air gets trapped in homes.
Strangely that comforts me. She asks me to open sweet peas
and then remarks that it's good to have one of "me" around.
I feel wanted. Heart's beginning to open. We wait for the
cab to pick us up to take us out to the airport. Until then...

2

The honeymoon officially begins when you finish your shower
and your partner hollers something like–"Sweetie, I got out
your denim jacket and sandals!" and after a radiant night
on The Costa Del Sol with paella and creamy cerveza you
wake up to the echo of wild coo-coos outside your terracotta
window you fathom are swallows from Africa; everything
forgotten in back pocket, your punctured bleeding soul and
punctual heart clogged (Egyptian dogs scuttling for iguanas)
and you wallow to morning buffet of goat's milk, almond milk
and pumpkin juice, hunks of cheese, honey cake and Pompadour Tea

3

To know your thief in pigtails who you are convinced
got for a steal; this was her subtle appeal brought up in
a neighborhood where they had the highest per-capita of
ADHD and Asthma, surviving and thriving in the blinking-
bone-marrow-neon forgotten-flashing-billboard-profile of
battered stars which rarely ever glowed; people from here

never even thought...too self-absorbed marching like soldiers
with Post-Traumatic Stress Disorder watching their backs
with heads held back literally planted over shoulder

4

Will fall asleep twitching to what she refers to as the "jimmies"
on the train barreling for Barcelona with guitar, classical-style
that snakes through the copper canyon, orange groves, and
gigolos fishing in jeans with no t-shirts on, off the cliffside
to The Mediterranean where whitewashed boats sail on by

5

The thick red crickets will begin the night
in the murderous streets of crazy candelabras
and lavish lovers and those wild parrots which
were convinced were peculiar mossy-green pigeons
stalking the street urchins and cosmopolitan citizens

6

Radiant Asian men wait patiently for customers outside
cafes along the emerald-green ocean where modern golden
metropolises shimmer and grace the sea and the closer they
seem the more it turns from a copper to a brass to a wheat

7

Erica sighs as she lies on top of my back
off the coast of Valencia making herself
perfectly comfortable, like the ultimate
neighbor-acquaintance-stranger; first time
I breathed and somehow found myself

completely contented inside this white
washed candy store where some old
Spanish woman out of the middle
of nowhere sells us fresh cashews
chocolate milko and move onward

8

Towards the flamenco
dancers and gypsies
and glass blowers

9

A humpback thief harasses the fake aristocrats
at the cafes both just as guilty for engaging
in this all too familiar fantasy and tragedy

10

In the morning in the countryside of Gandia
the sun squeezes through the canyon onto deep
red fertile planes where old men and their sons are
already out there and would never even think to complain

11

Erica and I get familiar in the bathroom of a rattling
rhythmic train where selfsame men in cappuccino suits
and powder-blue moustaches, crafted and chiseled with a
comical charm, smile and waddle back to ancient loved ones

12

Later on, I purchase a switchblade for 6 pesetas from some
sturdy Gypsy Spaniard, of which I cut *limons*, I mention
to my betrothed is no different than killing criminals
as the evening begins to bear fiery red fields turning
softer, finer, richer and warmer below purple geometric
hills of which you swear you see sparse silhouetted
solitary trees that resemble Picasso's vision
of Don Juan prancing in times of revolution

13

Through the window deer begin to glide along a golden
red gorge right below the iridescent lacy rim of the moon

14

There is no way to truly or accurately describe Spanish
women with their glowing chestnut, lost and romantic, faraway
eyes, timid and alive, subtle smile and blushing cheekbones
like the porous prisms of a rainbow, having been betrayed
having also survived, giving her depth, hung out to dry

15

In Sevilla, at the morning buffet, I hear Erica
say–"They were drinking champagne in suits.
I always feel awkward in my belly shirt…"

16

When the sun goes down, stuffy piano makes its way down
a staccato corridor where wealthy and whimsical accents
are paraded down hall and wonderful wax museum men from

Whales and stern German women sewn into armchairs, as
though wasted and deserted by culture, sitting sunburned
and drunken, going into their...10th, 20th, 30th year of
marriage when their roles and souls no longer make a
statement (as if they ever could) and catches up to them

17

While outside in the tree-lined darkening cafes of cobblestone
foreign women high on fine wine are torturing handsome young
waiters just trying to make a living to support their family acting
coy with feeble flirtation and vulgar innuendos. I sit on the head
thinking of what my late-great boss once said–"There's nothing
better in this life than a good bowel movement and six pack of beer"

18

Miraculous doves appear from midnight coast castle cathedrals
where veritable old timers literally roll kegs of beer
down cobblestone hills right around corners
and into the shadows of barrooms

19

Cultivating your own animal kingdom of giraffes with tentacles
Clams who crack knuckles peeping through drive-in seashells
Tiny little monkeys sprawled out on emergency soda crackers
Your wife who has become a peculiar and precious cuttlefish

Black cats who take out loans and now hang out in port-cafes
at dawn with sunglasses waiting for their ferries to Africa
or some Greek island. Dead dogs beg for spare change in
the corridor; Coca-Cola and charming Indian waiters who
grin and bear it taking orders for the aristocrats and hustlers

20

Last leg of the honeymoon sinking your teeth into deep
Greek pastry which gushes and trickles honey
down the steep white stairs to the sea

21

Gorgeous Greek maids fold feverishly in the pristine
white linen room of fine powders and perfumes
whisking you right back to the womb; how they
just sweep right into yours with shutters that open
to the sea, as widows' black schmatas wave in the
breeze. I wonder if there are any good memories
or just simply all betrayal and misery. Erica
sits on the sill like a silhouetted Siamese

22

Drizzle falls on the island as aging women sipping from
frosted iced coffee smile at cafes; the winds have finally
arrived off the Aegean Sea and I remain open for anything;
things never change much for me, seductions and wet welcoming…

23

The craziest chick I ever went out with finally revealed
all fervent and feminine secrets and fantasies and admitted
to me how much more horny were they than any…I just
smiled, took it all in, sighed and went to sleep

24

A herd of tourists follow jackasses uphill

25

In Santorini, we are lazy and nap during the day after
have mapped and wrapped up our destiny with a candle
in the sill, and there are bright blue chairs and shutters
of emerald and drift dreamily down cobblestone hills for
cho-co-late and sandwiches to a village in drizzle and maids
and stray dogs stroll past our window. There is a well and
widow and wife who gives you wicked stares in the mirror
after you make love in your bungalow, souvenir seashells,
word puzzles and just below way down the winding cliffside
where donkeys reside the cruise ship wails three times and
imagine the startled Asian and German tourists trampling
and tumbling for dear life suddenly *looking alive*

26

I love old couples who turn invisible at tiny tables
like stone statues and don't have a word to say
to each other and decide instead to knock down
bottles like bloated Buddha's who have turned
silent for absolutely all the wrong reasons

27

I'm enamored looking out to the deep blue
(*This is the best way to be shallow...*) to know
there really is nothing out there except for the ghosts
of ancient artists and gods who once trod the hallowed
heap of holy hills beneath shimmering sumptuous stars

28

Hercules whistling at all the fine Greek ladies

29

One wonders if not so long a long long time ago
a husband once scribbled to his beloved into the
rugged rock stone along the side of the road graffiti
that might have said something as simple as "I love you"
whether it be in Native-American, Aborigine, Egyptian,
Greek or Roman as he felt even though still very lost and alone
somehow at home to have someone to help to lighten his load

30

On this island the stray dogs are as well known as the natives
and for no particular reason will get up out of their stupor
to make their way around the corner towards ouzo and
peanut brittle windows to find some flaky tourist to pick on

31

Good daughters drive their contented demented olive-pickin'
fathers into town who proudly no longer give or take orders

32

These islands that now cast their omniscient shadows
onto a mysterious ocean in the breathtaking brilliant
shift of seasons like forgotten dusks of lost Americas

33

O to wake up in the morning to feel the billowy blue breeze
awaken your spirited being with a slow stream of schmaltzy
Greek strumming serenading some precipice like the wail
and whisper of ecstatic luscious seductive sirens from

34

just past the volcano twisting through the hollow wisp
of the naked islet to a final island of onyx and scarlet
ash sprouting from The Mediterranean somewhere
over that mysterious milky horizon with bare white
washed churches and villas slipping down the sculpted
cliffs and palm trees hovering like freewheeling fezzes
to the heavens and seagulls that soar and sail to the
magical endless ocean all in one subtle motion

34

This is where the Greek writers constructed their concept
of mythological gods that were transcendent and ageless
when the spare piano key stairs wind down to the tongue
of the timeless sea. This is the only way to exist embedded
deep within cats and cactuses hidden in the miraculous mist
of perfect nothingness; to hear the bells and clap of distant
donkeys make their way to the horizon and eventually vanish

35

The rough seas so raucous and redeeming, as fierce
and fragile as restless humanity, tenuously tragic with
movements that seem so slapstick and steeped in surviving
everyone appearing drunken, staggering, doing figure-eights
down the helpless hallway in a slothful fit of frenzy, saucers
flying and children are bawling; gigolos with sleeping masks
looking silly, cradled to the ceiling, steadily snoring; whole
families casually playing cards, chain-smoking and cracking
up collectively, cartoonish cackling; bursars and barbers
nimbly picking up and putting down phones dramatically

36

This is where you finally feel stoic and free, no longer having
to prove a thing, or to be anybody; these soulful, shipwrecked
thieves in thick, tinted glasses looking over the rail to the horizon
like real Aristotle Onassis' and their windswept widows cradled
in a culture of cobwebs based on some warped tradition and you
swear when the storm is over some lost lady comes up to you and
poignantly points her finger to some random island to offer "Atlantis?"

37

Back in Boston back in America
you read Camus in laundry rooms
convinced a huge box of cornflakes
will help to keep you from feeling blue

38

To suddenly and strangely return to a place replaced
by a secret palace of golden leaves, glowing and glistening,
growing, gathering, blanketing and bathing your charming
little Cape in a blank shaft of beauty and in the evening
one witnesses the hushed silhouettes of this brilliant
menagerie where there is a natural synchronicity
which sends a breeze brushing through trees
sinking right into your being with the whispering
of wind chimes, chattering and chuckling and
tickling your sensibilities tucking us into fantasy

39

Her breathing was like the wheeling winds and tides
of ripe and restless ages that helped to decipher all
that acquired madness which separated rage from estrangement
rhetoric from experience; the natural strange course and cycle

of loneliness that penetrated every pour of your existence as
you fell back into slumber to once more capture and celebrate
the clear and concise rhythms of radiant emptiness where
everything once haunted turns transcendent and timeless

40

Only to be awoken in the morning by some murmuring
monstrous machine sucking up all those skittering leaves
leaving simply a puddle of spooky foghorns blowing branches
with a gleaming golden carpet of antiquity outside the courthouse
of civility when dairy trucks doing their rounds rattle by routinely

41

Time is counted
by New England
Lighting Company

42

A radioactive ladder leans luminously against the beams
of some barren blustery bridge left for autumnal spirits
who still ponder the difference between truth and image

43

This is the perfect season for reflection
when seagull turns to crow to dove to vulture

44

This is what I remember and this is what I'll always cherish
the subtle and eternal cycle of seasons (misunderstood and
abandoned picked up by leftover, tragic women outside
matinee movie theaters; the stray scent of your homesick
sandwich waiting for a school bus beneath towering
leaf piles in a drizzle that seemed to last forever)

45

Those bus stops that will forever remain etched in your
imagination as we used to sway like *Boo-dah* with hair
of weeping birch branches and hearts of smoldering,
scarlet forests, swaddled, huddled, and holy entranced
with the self-determined rhythms developed from
a damaged culture simply waiting for someone
or something to pick us up for supper

46

That brooding Buddha who'd sit lotus-style with a wilted
flower and corn pipe in jaw humming heartfelt mantras
alongside the empty crowded curb waiting for The Lord
or some other misty-marquee-god to suddenly appear and
deliver him to his dazzling distant door like a scarecrow
stuffed with silky straw right below the moon and stars

47

Looking like the funeral director who has his palms
perfectly, politely and patiently prepared, planted
behind his back beneath the clock tower in a field
of corn where the flickering neon of some diner never
fails to remind us all about "Pancakes and Chili Dogs"

48

The mysterious silhouette of svelte sisters
with wild whipping hair disappearing in the
brutal and blissful dusk of whispering years

49

You now refer to her
as your *little monkey*
as you kiss her angel
toes in the morning

50

Wiggling like a mermaid's
tail which just happens
to surface every so
often without warning

The News

I found out she was pregnant when we
both worked at that mental health clinic
her with the adult team and myself with
the children's team and experienced that
spiritual, physical phenomenon where it
feels like you are literally 'walking on air.'
The only other time I felt that before was
when I heard that really cute girl from the
grade below me liked me and swear nothing
felt better. Just after lunch she gently knocked
on my office door and almost in a state of blissful
shock and awe told me how the nurses told her
in town; she couldn't believe it and bought like 3
or 4 more tests all of course with the exact same
results. When I had supervision just a little bit
later, my supervisor felt the need to proudly
show off his watch his wife just bought him
for the holidays (as he had repeatedly done
in the past like when I had been put on a case
and finally cracked open had had a cop confess
during family therapy to pedophilia and it being
in the paper of course not really giving a damn
and his instant response competitively like
some pathetic sibling rivalry was to whip
out an article about him in his drawer; this
was my source for support and validation)
and with a grin just having gotten the news
about my wife's pregnancy told him how nice
I thought it was, while realizing at that exact
moment, like some sort of ironic revelation
what an idiot he was, as already simultaneously
walking on air suddenly made aware it's all
just really about the little things and details
in this thing we call our time on earth

While Counseling

I was messing
around with this kid
asking him like I always
did what happened to his freckles
and if someone had stolen them and
he responded with the most sincere
and straight-faced kind of expression
reminding me of why I got into the profession
that probably they fell off him and ran down
the road and jumped onto someone else's nose
when I got a knock on the door from one of
my other little men who simply stood there
as though feeling honored to deliver some
life or death message like the whole world
depended on him with such a heartfelt passion
as if proudly looking up to a flagpole–
"You have an emergency phone call"

It Seems

"as though
we're gonna
have to get him out"

The Lactation Lady

made mention
Erica's breast milk
was like liquid gold.
To me it looked a lot
like that custard you
get stuffed in the middle
of Boston Cream donuts
at Dunkin Donuts during
childhood and if for that
and that reason alone it
is liquid gold I make
sure every last drop

gets into the bottle
then shuffle with
gusto on our daily
ritual across Dr. Zhivago
snowdrift mysterious dusk
blizzard park in Providence
dark with liquid gold inside pocket
to deliver precious parts to Dylan

Dainty Creatures

who swaddle
& cradle &
feed mother
milk bottles
so feminine
& maternal
not even
related
simply kind
& careful
gracious
caregivers
with a sense
of humor &
sense of honor

Returning Back To The Lullaby

to the frankfurter boiling
to the fish sticks baking
icy scenes accumulating
outside living room window
to silhouettes of a bleak
empty suburb developing
their own pure ripe mythology
restless rivers raging through
pachysandra silence penetrating
the core of your senses healing
the sadness, rage, pain, misery

nourishing your dreams
feeding the most acute
part of the anatomy
daffodils will
soon be ready

Faith

Sometimes don't it seem
like the scene is waiting
in the foghorns & rain for
a bus you know will never
come your way, wondering
what happened to all those
heroic friends, thieves &
comedians, father figures
lovers, the perfect night
for quahogs & chowder
rueben by the incubator

Moliere

What happened
to the real
life actors?

Dylan

How strange it must be
your first week of living
I can't even begin to fathom
what you must be thinking...

Well don't...

Leave that all to me
and simply just be
leave all the worrying
to Mommy & Daddy

Elevator Machine

Weird men in radioactive goggles
sneaking lemon meringue pie
to their secret laboratories

I wish I was one of those
peculiar men with a little privacy
and some purpose and meaning in this life

Industry Of Religion

Pompous punch lines of penguin
looking pastor in the solarium
whose sarcasm appears similar
to some sober drunken bum
& when he's all done
seems empty & solemn

Human all too human

as Nietzsche might say
in no way shape or form
meant in a flattering way

Dusk At Hospital

Finally the smoke
stacks & steeples!
The pine trees!

It seems as though
I haven't seen land
for a whole eternity

Those Days

I was so alone
living alone
way out on
the West Coast
and on occasion
might occasion
the strip clubs
on some bleak
Sunday afternoon
not knowing a living
breathing soul and take
off when those strippers
just seeming to go through
the motions would methodically
shake their bony asses & would
lose instant interest & no
longer felt turned on
while this seemed like
the sad lonesome desolation
of the misty maddening ages and
return back to my brokedown hotel
beneath bridges with some prison
bus suspended in darkness slowly
drifting over sleepy colonials
of dark sleepy towns of America

Aftermath Of Blizzard

In the morning all the universe
contemplating, hypnotized
over their tea & coffee
thinking about what
the day will bring

Construction workers in Nice
the railway workers on strike
in Italy, nomads of The Bronx
sweet suburban nurses, book
clerks and their thieves

Looker

Snow geometrically melting
forming in between the folds
of the roof of an old colonial
on top the crescent of *China Moon*

Male-Oriented

Dylan was discovered
to be the one responsible
for lifting the jewelry
of all the pretty nurses
it was believed while
during the stage of "burping"
and secretly stuffed all the loot
beneath his swaddling blanket.
Of course he vehemently
denied all this and started
poignantly pointing his finger
at Mommy as I must say it is
uncanny how much he takes
after Daddy while this must
also explain all the smirking
in his Little Bo Peep sleep.
It is also important to note
that he was caught winking
into the incubators of The
Godfrey Twins in which they
had no other choice but to put
him on a strict behavioral plan
where the doctors were found
to demonstratively demand—
"Just behave yourself!" It was
discovered just a little while
after this meeting that there
was one broach, school pin,
and engagement ring missing

The Littlest Sneeze Of All Time

They told me your name
means son of the sea
satisfactorily sipping
from your spring
of liquid gold
& whenever
we ask how
you're doing
you subtly crack
a secret smile
that delicately
curls from upper
lip all the way
up your cheek
as though getting
a real kick out of
worrying your parents
at such a young age.
I get a kick out this
too baby because I was
exactly the same way
people telling me you
resemble me, go figure?

Reflections From The Solarium

*

All is brutal & fruitful
like milk & honey
that is why we take
trips out to Italy, Sicily
an eternity of ejaculating
fresh olive & cocoa from
rugged god-like mountains
taking ferries back to
the mainland at dawn

*

What is it about that flashing traffic light
whether it be the desolate & beautiful
snowy vacant lot autumnal town
subtle seduction of Spring
or tragic & sultry Summer of twilight
that gets us to start sincerely thinking?

*

All those stray days hiding away
in the blessed redemptive rain
haunting the 2 dollar theaters
on the outskirts of Portland.
All those roles. All the hustles.
All those hotels. *The Jack London*
for example where you read piles & piles & piles
of novels. Poetry & philosophy from donated blood
& bone marrow. All your sorrowful travels watching
the sun rise in the mountains from second & third jobs
returning home just as solemn literally not being able
to afford to take a thing for granted wearily shuffling
over bridges. Over rivers. Back to your hovel with a
breathtaking view of the alley where an old Jewish boxer
simply swept up silently. The ultimate metaphor for mortality

*

After the soul-searching is over
you find yourself *discovered*
and the only thing leftover
(which you consider to
be eternal and forever)
is to feel mildly contented
solemn, numb to culture

*

Breaking down my later adolescence
it sounded a lot like–"Fuck you!
You're the one with the attitude!"

*

I love how they express themselves
out in these parts of New England.
How they refer to felines as "inside"
or "outside" cats. Sometimes I wonder
if in fact I had the chance to be an
inside or outside person what would I choose
yet I don't have to really think too long or hard on
that and know for sure what is false and what is true

*

Taking long warm suppers getting closer to Erica
rekindling the romantic flame in cul-de-sac cafeteria
(a lot of sighs & punchlines, fries & Boston cream pie)
with whole courtyards, patio furniture, garden walls &
dwarf birches engulfed, swallowed in the mythology of snow

*

Her telling me about her best friend
from The Boogie Down named Ann Margaret
Mary Farley Furlawn who used to protect her
and beat up bullies and say such things like–

"Hey kid give me your lunch money!" and how
in elementary she was the understudy to the giant
blueberry in Willie Wonka and the Chocolate
Factory having lost out to Suzie Seltzer
I guess was a little more convincing

*

Returning back to your reality
which was everything you dreamed
of in the brutal beauty of ball field
in holy-moly cruddy cruel rain of Winter
literally hearing your heart beating alone
with the muffled roar of the crowd and winds
sifting through distant pine trees; the melancholy
mirth of some sobbing sopping earth magically melting
first brush and run-in with palpable spirit of mortality.

Back then in the suburbs you always seemed to be hurting
too often, heart breaking too frequently, returning home
all bruised and battered for hot showers, suppers, and
slumber, a cool coin collection you gathered from
field trip out to Philadelphia stored in a safe little
safe with a hidden bag of bb's and secret love
letters from second cousin out in California
leaving room open for action & adventure
imagination, possibility, and promises

The Human(e) Anatomy

Keep soul
holy whole
drink midnight
milk when you
feel globs of guilt
down in the dumps
lower than low
beacon in the kitchen
the great ghostly glow
fragile tragic folklore
which eroded away ego
brainwashed & borrowed
from so long ago
so far away
from home
then let it all go
let it all glow

& once more flow
forgive & give
yourself freedom
to grieve & grow
like a river
like a rose
dreams shall tell all
the ones when you sleep
the ones when were poor
the heart surely knows
mind's bit of slow poke
a tired old bore
which tippy-toes
and snores
yet if you can just
give it the chance
the romance
from before
may follow like
a kind old man
or stray dog
whose eyes
tell you the
difference
between
right & wrong
what it's like
to be loyal
to belong
to be holy
whole whole
to be ready
to be reborn

Art Of Philanthropy

Erica blowing
purple bubbles
in parking lot
(not obnoxious
but nonchalant)

I find myself
falling in love
with her all
over again

Reasons Why I Love Her

Because she'll hit you with certain choice comebacks
like–"You and your black & white documentaries...
Subtitles...The Kennedy's...Peru...Cuba...
The rise & fall of the Eyebrows..." while you
find yourself cracking-up in the nook of her neck–
"What are you talking..." and escape the room pretending
to be pouting and her still continuing to give it to you–
"Cry me a river...Machismo boy!" as all you can really do
is bow your head and ask her if she wants anything from down
in the kitchen feeling honored to be like one of those straight
men in some *Three Stooges* comedy I mean you tell me what
girl do you know who can really keep up with Larry, Moe
and Curly, all upbeat Spring Training in about 6 weeks

A Cold One

I miss the old timers
from Brooklyn who
whenever there'd
be a blizzard see
them dragging
cases of beer
a whole other
William Carlos
Williams in their
little red wagons

Step Down

At last we finally
follow the stars
from Providence

to New Bedford
a new bed for Dylan.
The doctors & nurses
said when he got there
he instantly ripped out
his feeding tubes and had such
a firm grip he wouldn't let go
of their fingers. They seemed a bit
shaken. Erica looked like a new woman
calm, centered, and contented. She was
and thought perhaps I'd follow in her footsteps
and she wore this pretty periwinkle scarf draped
over her sweater. I've never seen her look better.
And share a nice Chinese meal around the kitchen
table, laughing a little on how when she first met
me I still had bags that had not been unpacked from
vacations all filled with maps and books from Central
America, and when she did unpack them, how I casually
responded–"O, I was wondering what happened to that
one and so on eliciting the comment–"I should have known
right there and then." A little later on the moon looked like
some ethereal cradle as I found myself welling up within
my window. Seemed as though I had not felt that kind
of passionate sort of love in ages…

Upon Returning

When I asked if there was anything new
which had gone on since I was gone
it was the same kid who went on

How he had found he would
be living in a new home as his
eyes lit up when he described

The place that was so large
it had like a 100, 1,000
1,000,000 doors…how

He was going
to be moving
into the home

Of a
million
doors

Can't Wait

For Dylan
to see his
new digs

His own
bassinet
own crib

One Day To Hear

A chorus of goo's & ga's
soft sweet murmurs
that not even

A cricket, cicada
tadpole or frog
could mock

Some cherubic dolphin
whose carnival call
mystical & raw

blissfully plunges
into the deepest
recesses of heart

Year Of The Fox

These days Dylan
listens to Cat Stevens,
Joni Mitchell, Peter Gabriel.
They say he's going through
some stage now of smiling. Is
there a stage in which you simply
stop smiling? And if so, why not just
throw on a little Cat Stevens, Joni Mitchell
Peter Gabriel. Erica readjusts her toe ring...

Sensing Shadows

Stilts to the lagoon risen
as all is finally forgiven.
Filthy sheep ramble
through wildflowers
of the apothecarian

"Mopey!"

And you look
forward to those
days when you may
be a toothless old man
and crow at the crows–
"Get away from my crocuses!"

That's when you
know you've
truly come
full circle

Like Mad Angels

Today I walked one of my kids
to the schoolyard for his session.
It was a nice day in New England.

And he proceeded to put his hand deep
in his pocket and pull out a gingerbread
man and declare–"I got this in church!"
then bit off his head and ran like a beautiful
blissful lunatic with his tongue hanging out
a stray leaf falling off a tree in the breeze
and tried everything, hopscotch, four square
had me time him racing back and forth from
fence to fence, groan of throbbing muffled
train whistle in the distance, and after his
fuzzy hair and freckles and fine face were
flushed and he had had enough and declared
without warning completely randomly that
when he turned seven he had stopped having
nightmares I took him back to the scent
of a luscious trail of fish sticks streaming
from the cafeteria (the echo of "we shall
overcome" of poised & polite students
over recorders in the distance) as he threw up
his hand and waved goodbye, then slipped
into the coat closet, snuck to his tiny
desk, and joined in with other fellow
classmates for an earnest recitation
of bluebirds. When I returned home
later that evening with eyes burning,
mouth sulking, I took my bambino in my
arms like Brando cradling his baby grandson,
wife dead asleep in the shadows, sound of crickets
whistling through our window, and thought if
I could die right now I'd die a happy man
and so might just make plans for tomorrow

13.

my greatest rapport is with the birds
who suddenly reappear every year
after the long winter and watch the
snow gradually start to disappear
filling up the rivers and bringing
life and character to the village
along with them scouting out the
lawn for specimens after having
spent their season in the warm
humid jungles of the rainforest
down in central america
for me they are always
welcome and a literal
blessing in disguise
and breath of fresh
air as they return
like long-lost gods
after having been
gone for so long
unaware of how
much you truly
missed them

proof:

coming back for new season
outside snowdrift crabapple
with mad spirit like that
bucktooth sister from
next door during
childhood over
split rail fence
in backyard

proof:

woodpeckers
with their mating
calls banging their
bills pecking on
back of the barn

proof:

bird sitting on wire contemplating looking out to the horizon
like one of those ole time brave and courageous explorers
on the cover of a text book in manifest destiny amerika

14.

courtyards! courtyards! courtyards! courtyards! all i dream of are those dreamy breezy transient courtyards from back in the day and whoever should make their way to & fro whether peer acquaintance, or stranger, i would always be fond of for all those fleeting escapist thoughts and lost reasons to be a part and not a part of...

15.

why does the long-winded analogy and metaphor always seem to drag on so much longer than the original story and moral until you feel just want to be left the hell alone even if it just means leftovers

16.

those who love to make those cliche claims
like "you only live once" as if that might help
to make things a little bit better, as i was not
asked to be born in the first place (motherfucker
mind your own business as who was even asking?)

17.

often when we deconstruct and analyze certain phrases,
expressions, and statements, such as the declaration–
"nothing personal" it does not come by coincidence
the individual in which it came from and emanated

18.

guys seem to just talk about themselves all the time
and never show any interest or curiosity in people
around them, which does seem in my opinion to
lack maturity, rather incomplete and fragmented
while women on the other hand if you get lucky
a little more depth and substance and compassion

proof:

i keep on getting from facebook *anna smith spark*
"new friend suggestion" sounds like the beautiful
ex red head of my ex best friend who was an
alcoholic who used to always just have these
erratic outbursts claiming all these girls were
looking at him (and got really mad and frustrated
if i didn't instantly agree and validate him and became
like some sudden out-of-control come-to-life phantom
having no idea where this all came from) when i never
even mentioned it, and always just seemed completely
out of context and kept on barking with these delusional
rants (like some napoleonic complex in action) they were
looking at him, while i was thinking what a dr. jekyl and
mr. hyde schmuck under the influence and couldn't even
be satisfied and content with this beautiful red head rich
daughter on lexington, who gave practically everything
to him, and i finally figured probably eventually wasn't
giving it to him due to these impossible embarrassing drunken
explosions (while i remember feeling how much more i liked
and felt sympathy for her and how he just didn't deserve her)
whining and complaining how she wouldn't sleep with him
and there were always these very logical sober reasons which
came out in self-pitying proclamations trying to make himself
out some poor martyr, as you'd finally realize and wonder…
and she was about as nice and pretty as they come so
you know maybe might just now consider becoming
friends with anna smith spark who sounds alot like
that girl with the flowing red hair on lexington...

19.

you and your damaged shattered pretty young girl
friend with the fiery red hair picking up wasted
vagabonds hitch hiking along the midnight sea
exchanging stories taking those long slow bleary
eyed trains of enlightenment suddenly awoken
out of your stupor from the holy sacred steam
of denver to chicago paris to nice the big easy
rattling through those deep southern swamps
at dawn back to patterson and new york city

20.

why when you're on top of the world
still feels like you're at rock-bottom
like a bum being picked up off the
sidewalk in front of the wine & spirits
shop by the owner and suddenly remarks
with a fine sense of humor–"top of the morning"

trauma stays with you like taking a fine fresh shower
while having to put your dirty stinky rags on again…

21.

i think my first instincts
when i was a wise ass kid
were the realest and most relevant

everything thereafter felt like an interview
where you knew the questions before
they were gonna even ask them…

proof #1

his parents moved them to the wealthy suburbs
for purposes to get a much better education
(referred to it as "highly competitive")
but the only thing strangely ironically
learned was how they become adults
at much earlier ages and not much
of a childhood and what best friends
will do to you and still trying to figure

proof #2

how mean and cruel certain kids become
in the slums of suburbia and will desert and
abandon a friend they grew up with without
providing a single word or explanation because
they absurdly want to be accepted and turn to
some new and 'cool' clique (will do this without
remorse or contrition, and to be 'popular;' even
saying it has something of a strange and obscure
ridiculous ring to it, and will brutishly sacrifice and
scapegoat at their expense) while that good-hearted
and innocent kid (at way too young of an age) learns
about the brutal, erratic, hypocritical, and unjust nature
of mankind (neither men nor kind) and the adult world
made to self-loathe and feel small, guilty and conflicted
(that they did something wrong to deserve this) stunned
traumatized and damaged even without being aware of it
while becomes something of a cruel irony due to someone
else's completely poor and parasitic, mean-spirited character

proof #3

almost like some fucked-up backwards
proof of prove that you (don't) exist...

proof #4

sometimes identifying and realizing you have changed
context(s) and environments can help to reduce slightly
the damage and trauma, while it will in no way fully solve
the full problem but perhaps can provide that spark or stepping
stone towards a sense of calm or possible light at the end of the tunnel

proof #5

we can of course talk about that "police action" in korea...
the war which was supposed to last for only 8 weeks in vietnam
but i think in my opinion and believe this strongly the generation
we never ever quite spiritually recovered from was the eighties
(which stole the soul of this country) and gave birth to that whole
horrible breed of yuppie, which was apparently young people in their
20's to young 30's who didn't feel very young to me, greedy, soulless,
somehow treated like royalty and about as mediocre and uncreative...
who were just out for self and to make a quick buck whoever it was
and whoever's throat got cut, and could never ever really relate to
and felt instantly alienated; kids graduating from high school (already
having their whole lives plotted and planned for them, like some very
safe ship sunken in a bottle up on the mantle) as all they were thinking
of was a very competitive college (then business school) as a stepping
stone for some top-notch stock firm, and how they could make quick
money by taking advantage (even if it meant cheating at all costs)
on their fellow man they referred to with such business-like terms
as leverage or purchasing bonds or selling short and never under
stood any of that lingo or for that matter, friends i thought i had
known just a very short while ago...

proof #6

i could never be a conservative cause they seem like aliens
from another planet (who make alienating and 'ostracizing'
a daily habit) but sometimes i swear find these so-called
liberals to be just as guilty in being judgmental and exclusive
(speaking in absolutes and all too quick in making sweeping
generalizations) while in their own way come off awfully
hoity-toity and pretentious with their passive-aggressive
opinions and know-it-all intellect which can also be viewed
(rigid and insular) as not particularly open-minded or receptive
and if broken down empirically even with hostility and prejudice

proof #7

it's always been bullshit and hypocrisies
and a complete lack of truth and justice
(beyond belief and virtually impossible
to comprehend or fathom) that has
broken me down but in fact looking
back to their behavioral patterns know
it clearly as their complete lack of character
(and moral fiber) and something in the long-run
of a blessing in disguise if you get where i'm coming from

proof #8

do we all have to be grandiose and full of shit
just to make it? in fact it's always been doubt
and conflict that's gotten me out the door...

proof #9

with all that back and forth bickering shit
they become the core of situational depression.
there was that scene in that jim jarmusch movie
"down by law" where tom waits' girlfriend kicks
him out just no longer really inspired or motivated
anymore and all he really cares about is like getting
his guitar and extra polished shoes from under the bed

proof #10

when those dudes made it to the moon
there was this historical claim they were
such brave courageous heroes (and they
probably were) but it's my estimation too
they were just probably trying to escape
(the blues and had nothing to lose) and
paid their dues and needed the downtime
to get away from planet earth a life of leisure
and the madness of what marriage does to you

proof #11

wow how they all just drain you
to the point of complete nausea!
married life is alright, but like
to keep the window open for ol'
friends from childhood to crawl
into i mean the real ones of youth
way before that phase of puberty
of gossip and rumors and betrayal

still trying to find a place with good
pork fried rice up here in the mountains

proof #12

it's a strange phenomenon but often
during the warmer months i like
to picture and imagine the holidays
and like some nice kind docile dog
just passed-out dozing-off in front
of the fire perhaps lapping up a bit
of the eggnog or having sniffed out
the stash of marijuana in rich son's
drawers going at it gobbling it all up
and becoming a part of the punchline
for his pals not a whole heck of a lot
he can do about it cause can't really
tell his parents his dad a guy we really
liked always smoking that stubby cigar
one of those cut-throat lawyers in new
york consistently on and off with getting
separated and mom driven mad driving
like mad like some madwoman taking
us to see the rangers at the garden but
all's good cause able to keep that
numb high for like a couple days
straight in a fine daze looking out
contemplating over all those seasonal
brooks and clocktowers of the suburbs

there's a reason you dream of
christmas during the summer

proof #13

imagine
getting an e-mail
still thinking of you
still jerking off to you
wonder if would feel
flattered or just pressured
(lose respect) and get scared
off similar to how the original
relationship started and ended

been watching alot of steve mcqueen
and ali macgraw movies these days…

proof #14

sometimes just doesn't feel
like home until things broken

proof #15

life like those shattered bottles
after school in the schoolyard
those paint-by-number murals
made up of a variety of blues

proof #16

you turn to art when things turn away from you
there's a tabby cat tip-toeing in the belfry of the steeple

incestuous cousins in a rowboat entering the lagoon…

proof #17

that classic *i love lucy* episode where she
innocently repeated over and over—"slowly
i turned, step by step, inch by inch…" which
became this instant psychological trigger for
this slapstick schtick to suddenly spray a seltzer
bottle right in her face and no matter what she said
or how she resisted couldn't stop him or get past it

proof #18

"alfred tickle novelty co."
parking for the pastor only

in periods of great frustration
we ask the hypothetical question
when will it ever end yet what might
prove to be far more accurate is did
it ever begin? the escape artist has
uncanny chameleon/impersonator-
like abilities which he picked up at
a very young age naturally learning
to cope and survive a tormented reality

proof #19

so who would really want to live happily ever after?
it just doesn't even sound right, as all just seems like
some flimsy fly-by-night scam or unbelievable fable
invented by the con-artists and false raconteurs who've
never seen it and wouldn't know what it was or looked
like even if it hit them so the thing to always remember
is that it is all simply fleeting and comes in momentary
flashes during those very rare periods when you least
expect it not experiencing pain and suffering and just to
dig it and be contented from a zen-buddhist perspective

proof #20

who would want to devote a whole existence
worried about reputation seems like a complete
waste of life in acting and overcompensating

the personification of missing-in-action...

proof #21

picture some dope addict eternally nodding-out
over the holidays in front of the jerry lewis telethon…

22.

thinking back to lunch at the school cafeteria
didn't it always just seem like fries
with way too much ketchup?

23.

girls in high school used to worship themselves
while interestingly ironically boys said a prayer
that would usually go unanswered but if by some
stroke of luck or miracle it was declared (and put
out there) that she liked you was walking on air
and felt like for the first time ever you existed
and did everything humanly possible to try
and make this persist and feeling last forever

24.

looking back at my life all hope and happiness
was that social we had with that girl's summer
camp across the lake, and holding the hand
of debbie schultz that really cute girl from my
hometown, whose long brown chestnut hair
flowed down her bosom (that strange stage
of puberty growth & development where
they start off flat-chested and come back
complete women having blossomed like
some holy pop-up photosynthesis) roller
skating round and round and round and
round the social hall during the disco era
entranced, enraptured and nothing could
have felt better, more romantic, more a
sense of belonging, building up a sweat
rollerskating for hours on end our own
version of living happily ever after not
caring what would happen (which is
the finest form of 'time standing still'
in existence) when finally returning
home somewhere at summer's end

proof:

i remember hearing dawn sommantico
reading *the battle of the light brigade*
in high school english class in that
slow soft hypnotic cadence and being
put right under her spell and after each
stanza repeating the refrain–"enemies
to the left, enemies to the right, and then
came the 600" having no idea what the
hell she was saying and what any of that
meant but didn't give a shit and couldn't
care less as thought (or wasn't thinking at
all) this is what it must be to be instantly
in love and under the influence of some
girl or some love drug like opium like
when you first get high drinking way
too much *manischewitz* wine on passover
night or the first time you get drunk at a keg
party and able to charm all the girls with some
of the craziest and most clever shit of all time
having no idea what you said but apparently
enough to get them into bed–"enemies to the
left, enemies to the right, and then came the 600"
and all that wine, more like dawn sommantico
with that fine, romantic, sing-songy voice…

25.

you first got laid
by that nice catholic
school girl across the way.
you were a jewish boy from
back east while that time
to me in the big easy
true culture & diversity

26.

when i used to work at *commuter book centre*
right in the middle of the madness of grand
central station and all those madmen and
crack heads and commuters would just
come in for pretty much the same reason
just as desperate and miserable with pretty
empty lives looking to be saved and slowly
dying (having browsing down to a t) while
there was this young black lady who would
come in every so often literally to visit me
who we both loved alfred lord tennyson
and guess having this in common both
kind of ended up having feelings for each
other and look back to those interludes
and moments which meant the world

women literally clawing and fighting
each other at the postcard carousel…

27.

when just get sick of all that dumb fucken bickering
draining the hell out of you out of all things domestic
(which to me seems like a form of domestic violence)
or the whole marriage thing you think of calling
that nice sweet representative at the furniture
place or the bank always got something nice
and sweet to say and not for sleazy reasons
but just to see how life and things are treating
her (treating me?) and got the voice of a dove
i suppose like good ole mademoiselle edith piaf
to fall back on fall back in a deep sleep the big
sleep in my easy chair and get discovered like
jim morrison in his bathtub with a deadpan
grin in a complete state of relaxation having
finally at last 'broken through to the other side'
no longer tormented bothered incarcerated by life

28.

that sweet angel who reads right off her telemarketer
script and fills in the empty spaces to try and heal all
the empty spaces and holes in your broken heart and
broken existence yet more so prefer when she just acts
natural (and that, o manipulative and brainwashed pre
manufactured amerika when i'm really able to make a
connection) and tells me with great spirit and exuberance
she's not so far from me and tells me exactly where
she's from and i tell her i know exactly where she is
and able to instantly reminisce (of course mostly to
self) all those romances along route 7 in the berkshires

29.

i know i really love her cause
just a day after her emotional
outburst just thinking how sad
and mad she actually got (while
just thinking about that makes
me hurt) when she used to aim
the bottles straight at my head
and now know how much she
really cares cause through all
her sadness and tears could
see her going out of her way
to throw them the opposite
way while no matter how hard
it might get just will never forget
and would walk down the aisle
with her a thousand times again

30.

i don't know if it's just me but find
it rather interesting and depressing
and not sure if it just comes by coin
science or part of speech how the
card players keep on saying to the
dealer–"hit me!" while they keep
on losing to know living the fast life
is really just a way of slowly dying

while all i ever cared for was one
night with her sleeping by my side

31.

sometimes my life
just feels like the
projectionists are
on strike and no
one tells me about
it while i'm one of
those fleeting flashing
images up on the screen
and no matter how much
i scream or try to keep
it all in somehow seem
to be losing the light
turning all color
to black & white

A Thieves Cookbook For Coping & Surviving

1. add rusty nails to spice garden to help thriving

2. have mom bend wire hanger around puerto rican girl's belly
   to see how much she's growing on stoop during summer

3. make sure when lovers are strolling she walks on inside close
   to buildings as opposed to street to indicate she's not for taking

4. at wedding make sure to frisk and check for gun at door

5. put a raw chicken in crate and throw over the pier
   of coney island to catch crab and for supper
   add breadcrumbs & black pepper

6. for enterprising individuals holler all day
   by shore–"fudgie! fudgie! bud-wiza!"

7. put battery on shoulder and if
   knocked-off get ready as means war

8. for scraps after school have latino girls rub garlic on
   fingernails to scratch eyes out and make burn more

9. the rough & tough irish brothers who really love each other
   but will throw down practically anywhere throw out insults
   and doesn't matter where they are could be the inside of
   drugstore and so on will beat the crap out of each other

10. gangs having fist fights in *white castle* at midnight
    literally getting tossed through windows and being
    escorted in paddywagons chained around the ankle
    to destinations like bellevue & tombs & the next
    morning in the courtroom will find out their fate
    usually a 3-5 bid upstate at elmira, comstock, or
    attica without the help of al pacino & drag queen
    to melodramatically get them out on good behavior

11. during mother's day on a fine sunday one of the wise asses
    from the neighborhood in asphalt park while playing softball
    will sarcastically remark–"i see you're all spending the day with
    your moms" then when sliding into second pile on top of each other

12. center fielder easily distracted
    with absolutely no attention span
    scaling center field fence like spiderman

13. alpha-male macho man insulting effeminate drag queen
    and suddenly he/she kicking the shit out of him
    with broom handle used to play stickball

14. after playing hoop all day in tompkins square park
    in alphabet city hang-out with buddy in projects
    who shows me his 25 he keeps safely stored
    in *converse* sneaker box under his bed used
    purely for defense and those who offend

15. the stud from the neighborhood hanging-out on corner
    snaps at the cute girl returning home from work, who
    can't help but to smile and be flattered by his dialogue
    –"send me to the corner! i've been a very bad boy!"

16. the old timers from the social club pretending
    to hit each other over the head with wooden chairs

17. strange neglected kid standing on his head
    within the fence of his brownstone
    as if welcoming guests

18. one sign reads "confession" and the other "italian ice"
    both just as legitimate and helping to heal vice

19. ballerina deliberately hangs brassieres & panties
    on dripping clothesline as has a crush on guy upstairs

20. old lady married to nice & kind retired merchant-marine
    rubs olive oil from the old country into the aching
    belly of cat persistently pleading and purring

21. pit bulls planted on roofs trained to detect and sniff
    out the brave men in blue barking like mad when they
    show up in riot gear for their choreographed drug busts

22. taking baths with black girl in clawfoot tub
    whose father was a blind man from yonkers
    who owned a string of bodegas and eventually
    sent me postcards from san francisco telling me
    about the real bums so blue & down-in-the-dumps

23. chinese gangs boyfriends & girlfriends walking hand in hand
    reflective & introspective silent in leather from summer carnival
    midnight ferris wheel on delancey back to their tenements on hester

24. you look out naked exposed to the whole wide world
    from your top floor window on orchard over
    all the universe & steamy cobblestone

25. further south towards the brooklyn bridge, *gus' pickles*,
    religious artifacts, and ole time factories & sweatshops

where your ancestors are from and your great grandfather
every sunday strangely enough would bring your mom when
she was a little girl a full bag of candy and full bag of underwear

26. growing up our heroes were always people
    like oscar madison with that stained sweatshirt
    and khakis and mets hat turned around always
    with token beer in a can in a brown paper bag

27. while writing the sport's column
    in like that spacious seven room rail-
    road apartment overlooking park avenue

28. living the life of a bachelor
    with the *coo-coo* pigeon sisters
    when manhattan still had a middle
    class & midget wrestling & mad character

29. happily discovering stashes of divorced moms'
    marijuana stashed in night tables and as teenagers
    rolling them up with the sticks & seeds still in them

30. switching on the switch on the wall
    for a romantic electric fire for all

31. staggering bleary-eyed right around
    united nations with the sun rising
    to *bagel nosh* where could put
    practically anything on a bagel

32. getting into discos with fake id's
    and older girls secretly squeezing
    your tooshy and then disappearing

33. spending the rest of the evening
    trying to find them as in looking
    back what if in fact i did what
    would i actually say to them?

34. and this ridiculous journey
    which seems like the whole
    empty pathetic allegory for reality

35. rundown
    on-the-run
    the runaround

36. proudly excitedly explaining
    this to your pals never finding
    her with just a sad story to tell

37. spending sweltering summer evenings
    in new york city tossing eggs down
    on couples having candlelit suppers

38. in the courtyard
    and them stupidly
    surprisingly staring up

39. cartoonishly cracking-up
    and sneaking back
    into air-condition

40. rent-controlled studio for a bout of insomnia
    with sweat-stained sheets shivering worried
    about things acting-out without even being
    aware of it against figures of authority who
    had constantly bullshitted me & betrayed me
    & broke promises & beating them to the punch

41. watch angelic boys drop g.i. joe from ghetto windows
    with sisters blown-up tampons into alley of dead dolls

42. chase dope addicts back up fire escapes right where
    they belong and threaten to kill them if you ever see them
    again disappearing frightened like a flock of origami pigeons

43. wander through snowy sacred silent streets of brooklyn to russian
    supermarket from the old country to pick up your weekly dose of
    cheap chicken, booze, babka & babushka cookies written in slavic

44. return back reborn with a whole new outlook
    of sorts of subtle prayers & promises; mantras
    of echoing foghorns blasting down blessed alleys

45. listen to female roommates above you through paper-thin ceiling
    one a ballerina and the other an opera singer, sometimes belting
    soprano and when most down & out & lonesome getting familiar

46. do not have a single regret
    with any past girlfriend even
    if at times dramatic and high
    maintenance as almost always
    spiritual & intimate & provided
    an instant panacea & protection
    & escapism from the grueling
    & judgmental bullshit of everyday
    existence while pillow talk like private
    cathartic campfires getting rid of it all

47. watch melting snow flow like a revelation
    down gushing hills of cobblestone seeing seasons
    slowly shift outside *south brooklyn casket & alfred tickle co.*

48. tables & chairs being put out
    in front of mafioso social clubs
    transistors for oldies station & sports radio

49. the lines start to build up and get longer
    for *o.t.b.* & diabetic bakeries down the street

50. way out in the warm haze of one of those lazy days
    in queens at a corner bodega a boy reaches into
    a pull-out freezer and pulls out an italian ice in
    the shape of a pistol and just starts licking it

51. it's something of a well known fact that many of those
    who work on tugboats supposedly have filthy mouths

52. i suppose like when those lovely pork fried
    fish alleys start to heat up in chinatown right on
    the border of little italy and literal kung-fu theaters
    during the summer and turn stank during the season

53. in this half-crazed half-sane crackpot melting pot
    you hear a bouillabaisse of leftover dialogue like–

    the last time i was here
    the same mosquito bit me twice...

    that girl is just itching for some cock...

    i'd like a fries to go with that shake...

    sally in our alley...

    you could give a headache to an aspirin...

    all the way from bensonhurst, coney
    island, and madison avenue...

54. and can't help but to laugh a little to yourself
    only confirming how much really like a jungle
    and so much the difference between the sexes
    and genders, while these angels are almost forced
    to be flattered against their will caught somewhere
    on the fence between heaven and hell in the cut-
    throat field of publishing & advertising still
    driven trying to make names for themselves

55. those long last supper tables at the n.y. public library
    full of mad scholars & bums & winos leftover from
    the avenue somehow making their way into the
    windswept doors a great place to bide your time
    and lose yourself and figure it all out and try to
    make sense of it all veritably seeing the seasons

56. shed their skin from summer to autumn
    through the great big opaque windows
    where the bleary-eyed sun & shadows

57. seem dimmer but somehow more lucid & pronounced
    and after hours holed-down there strolling meandering
    and making your way back to your hovel on rivington

58. shadows grow longer from tenebrous branches
    off the mythological brilliant bridges & barges
    & skeleton skyline appearing to blink brighter

59. latin lovers in sky-blue suits at sunset
    carry electric roses to their mistresses

60. russian & polish widows show up to stoops
    at all hours of the night whose husbands like
    phantoms left them high & dry for all the
    right reasons both primitive & existential

61. while first born sons having overdosed on dope and
    now keeps guard over the garbage like stoic soldiers
    haunted foreboding making sure all tenants recycle
    and if not a hostile paroxysm of cold interrogation

62. wasted with jewish madman scholar from sheepshead bay
    brooklyn who had a thing for drag queens in the heat of the
    meat market in the west west village at the end of the world

63. whose mom used to beat him up and dad was a cop
    and therapist would get fed up and thrown out
    of sanctuaries in upstate new york

64. getting high off tablets of speed with ex-cons
    in the park chased by cups of coffee to keep
    the high going shots at *vazack's drinking tavern*
    in the lower east side and then making-out with
    black girls on harlem rooftops waking up the next
    morning not exactly sure where you were but that
    feeling like you felt like you belonged feeling
    that feeling of feeling a part of and reborn

65. the best places you can go to and roam around
    for air-conditioning is *bed bath & beyond* on
    6th avenue and just wander around soaking
    disoriented disassociating as if this actually
    was your own dream home somewhere in
    the future, the *barnes & nobles* on the same
    avenue self-educating yourself for hours with
    a frapuccino, trying to pick up your future wife
    returning home a bachelor, and the $2 theater
    in hell's kitchen camped-out there all day
    moving from movie to movie...

66. put cooling witch hazel onto burn you got at the pool
on pitt st. followed by a feast of black sausage & plantain
stuffed with chopped meat washed down with *coco-rico* soft drink
straight from the machine and that joint which just reads "spanish
& chinese" right on delancey huddled beneath the manhattan bridge

67. watch best friend from hoboken climb up the inside of the spine
of the girders at night of the williamsburg bridge and literally
leap over parts which haven't been filled in because of contracts
& corruption & organized crime constantly changing their mind
over that *span* of time

68. wonder why the union of doormen & custodians
get paid so much better than school teachers

69. pace yourself to get through the evening as a doorman
for your graveyard shift camped-out in bellman's closet
slightly open for the sleazy salesmen from the midwest
staggering in trying to sneak in unsavory guests nodding
out with your slice of stolen key lime pie from the kitchen
ezra pound's *cantos* kerouac's *desolation angels* like a religion

70. wake yourself up and rearrange the lobby which includes
primping pillows, unloading ashtrays, polishing brass handles
of luggage carriers, and putting up the letters for cosmetologist
and pharmaceutical conventions; like a phantom slipping bills
under guest doors

71. greet whole hoard of gorgeous puerto rican girls
to die for entering doors for housekeeping chores

72. bring in whole stack of morning papers, sweep up
outside in front of hotel and hose down curb, don't
forget to pick up luggage in hall for german & asian
tour groups and bring bags to bus

73. take subway home to brooklyn with great big ball
of blinding sun rising beaming & bouncing off of
navy-blue windows of drowsy red brick factories

74. stray dogs leaping & lunging & playing
grooming & cleaning themselves off
in the splashing waves by the shore

75. old black man literally in blue suede shoes
with a pair of headphones on leaned back
on a bench all alone on the boardwalk

76. those guard dogs of the used car lot
who used to go on the literal all-out
seething attack, as you'd share your
fried chicken bones with and became
your lonesome real-life man's best friend
all of us just standing there at the end of
the docks, at the end of the cobblestone
at the end of the world in red hook, brooklyn
brooding, contemplating, in the bare fresh air
of winter within the silhouetted snowfall just hearing
the clanging of buoys, like the far-off church bells of
the season while looking off solitary, holy to the ancient
opaque, delineated, and sentimental figure of lady liberty

77. morning mists burning off majestic bridges
connecting manhattan to the transcendent nostalgic
boroughs and new jersey, looking southward once
again to the statue of liberty, atlantic & old country
and up north where that brilliant miraculous hudson
rambles right past ulysses s. grant tombstone, young
teddy roosevelt mansion and into the expansive
adirondack mountains, which houses millionaires
& madmen, prisons & institutions in no man's
never never land of the forgotten & forgiven

78. old distinguished white-bearded black man with eyes of kindness
    & wisdom whose white girl walked out on him and left him in
    the park when used to give art exhibits at *the whitney & frick*

79. hookers & homeless & penniless hoteliers literally scrubbing-up
    with bars of *lava* soap and *gee your hair smell terrific* shampoo
    with fire hydrants opened up in a half-crazed hysterical commune

80. ghosts in 10th avenue hell's kitchen boxcar diner
    that part of the nightlife when city's
    most abandoned & silent

81. i was the moses child never picked up or discovered
    ironically thriving off a mistaken identity & instantly
    entered the blackmarket & vaudeville sweeping
    the sawdust & flour from the butcher & bagel
    shop to put food on the table & kept it all stored
    in the back of my mind during those graveyard
    shifts hustling a yellow taxi watching the city
    go down each & every night like the light
    exploding from a projectionist's booth
    always deathly alone with the bust of
    the moon over my shoulder taking my
    notes down on the receipt paper i swear
    really did this a trickster phantom former
    ghost of myself figuring it all out from
    the secret shadows & silhouettes of
    the trap door all the way to the catwalk
    & scribbling my name like glowing spiders
    on brilliant misty marquees just off off-broadway

82. if slumlords refuse to give you heat for the winter
    deduct it from the rent in existential increments

83. if slumlords refuse to fix your buzzer
    attach an extra key to sock and toss it out
    window watching it sail like a carrier pigeon

113

84. to survive the wild heat of a summer in brooklyn all you need
is a refrigerator full of milk & seltzer with leftover fried fish
& plantain & gizzard, multiple cold showers and stick your
head in the freezer, drop naked dripping to futon on floor
with your muted tv of edward g. robinson, bogie & bacall

85. cab crashed through café window on 3rd avenue
while pale-faced party girl coming off a night of
coke & blunts still mechanically serves blue plate
special & coffee on a bleary-eyed sunday morning

86. poor princess beneath parasol who works for *pierre-deux*
on lexington whose man tragically walked out on her gets
suddenly knocked over by a deaf boy doing sign language
resembling a busted tumbling umbrella blowing in the wind

87. when i first met fiancee we used to love to slow-dance
somewhere right around dusk in my railroad apartment
with a boxing bag hanging from the ceiling in that little
enclave around the heather gardens of cloisters with ultra-
orthodox jews and giggling puerto rican parochial school
girls at the bus stop while this transient and surreal
state of flux made you feel so alive in the present
and not worry so much about the future

88. she was still living with her mom in the bronx and whenever
her erratic mood swings would kick in and drive her up
the wall would just show up and was so young would
store all these trinkets and tchotchkes under my pillow
like some transitional-object still somehow trying to
make a sentimental connection and out of nowhere
fill my cupboards with stuff she temporarily took
from her mom and eating straight from the can
i'd wonder and ask where did this come from?

89. just trying to make it through and survive graduate school
at yeshiva to receive our masters for social work and internship
working with the schizophrenics under the el on jerome avenue

90. for sadistic discipline when inviting relatives over make daughter
kneel naked on rice in corner while balancing a bible on each hand

91. bring kid to movie theater and make him look down
at floor and avert eyes the whole time film's playing

92. put banner up made up of bed sheets swinging from apartment
building over city pool during sweltering summer to indicate
brother's returning home from upstate doing a bid for robbing
a whole string of *friendly's*

93. scribble haiku in twilight lower east side park
washed down with a quart of *ballantine*
way too hot in apartment and mom with
multiple children running over your head
nonstop and just never shut the fuck up

94. the dominican girl who you have a mad crush on
with the crooked front teeth which just makes her
look cuter senses this and picks it up selling papaya
and plantain at the fruit stand but in real life would
be a clash of cultures as rarely date outside their own

95. one of your best friends who's dominican as well
who i owe money to and says no problem don't
worry about it gets into a quarrel with a drug dealer
uptown put down on his knees execution-style and
shot in the back of his skull and just like that he's
gone and coffin shipped to the d.r. while dudes
from the neighborhood so casual and don't seem
to care at all and say he shouldn't have gotten into
it with him and more so shocked by their nonchalant

indifference and suppose as a defense-mechanism a-
long with everything else somehow turn numb as well

96. mourn for buddy who got shot and didn't even know
it cracking-up drunk on broadway on saturday night
with his small intestines hanging out of his insides

97. mourn for pal who suddenly got stabbed with a rusty screwdriver
in the middle of the park and the ambulance drivers showing up
going at it cause didn't have insurance and that hesitation
finding out he didn't make it the next day in the paper

98. mourn for martyr with an impossible to please father
who went to columbia university, an actuary with
bipolar disorder and got so depressed made a mad
dash for it leaping into the east river and reeling him
back in giving him the ultimatum of either electric
shock therapy or a long term visit and stay at bellevue

99. mourn for old girlfriend from hell's kitchen
who was a mafia princess and saw her step
brothers torture and murder so many victims
and eventually couldn't take it and did herself in

100. mourn for rich girl from michigan who claimed to be a zionist
whose father was a physician and sexually frigid, and seemed
to have more of a thing for him, professors in klezmer orchestras,
free samples at *zabar's*, pure pedigrees, and own private doorman

101. mourn for maddening girlfriend impossible to get close
to with an eating disorder and did everything i could for
her and every time i tried to save and rescue the more she
turned off and became hostile and was a professional clown
and when off her meds would holler and howl and toss vases
at studs flung from her window returning home from nightclubs

mourn the murder & mayhem of everyday living
where crimes of passion seem like a sense of forgiving
mourn the seasons what will never & one day always be
mourn the madmen & starving artist jesus & superintendent
the forgotten daughters who haven't been touched for ages
mourn all those poor girls who just miss their father figures
& guys who walked out on them so lonely all you hear
is long plaintiff wailing being drowned-out by showering
mourn all lost boys from oklahoma & brooklyn & baltimore
with everything to look forward to & nothing to look back on
& your thread of memories the only thing to live for
like some reel to reel projector at some long-lost theater
somewhere in the clitter-clatter between yesterday & the future

proof: not too far from descartes and jean-paul sartre

real true-blue existentialism is spending a whole existence
trying to find and discover (track down and examine) *the killer*
of our mind, body, and spirit (the proverbial heart and soul)
which can often as well be self-destructive, self-fulfilling, or
even suicidal ideations and tendencies, which gets triggered
ironically as much through a 'fear of success' as a 'fear of failure.'
the psychiatrists like to refer to the term or dynamic of "hitting
rock bottom" (while i always pondered how is this possible or
more simply put, how would one know rock bottom if down
there at rock bottom) sometimes before we can make any
clear or distinct improvement in our psychological functioning
(moods or behavior) which apparently comes often through
some primal urge, instinct, or coincidence, but if we truly
reflect and look closely enough (into this state of 'rock
bottom') there in fact is a clear, 'prodromal,' consistent
pattern both cognitive and behavioral where this constantly
appears to manifest itself (get aroused and repeated) when
paradoxically we are at our most keen, lucid, and profound
level of perceived freedom and 'open-minded' (ironically fragile
and vulnerable arousing one's 'existential' and nihilistic doubts
and fears and anxieties) which triggers certain forms and traits
and characteristics of asceticism (a core so empty and vacant
with the intrinsic will and self-motivation towards 'maintaining'
and a 'state of safety' and 'certainty' thus attempting to enact
specific even 'dysfunctional' coping and survival mechanisms
and rituals, an 'innocent victim' stuck in the middle of the 'fight
or flight syndrome') the only reality we know (often acquired by
some past experience of psychological or spiritual damage) while
simultaneously, selfsame denial of this strange, obscure form of
a sudden, unfamiliar feeling of "happiness," as our self-image and
self-doubt (and fears) just does not allow or know what to make of it

32.

bluebird keeping an eye
on me through my blinds
not sure whether i want
to live or die digging in
to wife's *la choy* chicken
with peas & yellow rice
always likened myself
to something of a
renaissance man
sitting right in front
of the world news
with swollen rivers
growing outside
my window due
to the melt off
of winter and
beat down
and blue

proof:

baby bluebird hopping
through morning dew
of pussy willow…

first one to make
it through winter

proof:

where do the swans sleep at night?
(o! the broken bones of life!)

33.

what if after we go we find out it's all
just one big fucken game show and
like some repeat episode of life are
presented with taking what's offered
to us or what's behind one of those
big colorful glossy sequined curtains
and realize you just don't fucken
want any of it at all and want to
just be left the hell alone (don't
want to play the feud or make a
deal) and want to be as far away
as possible from human creatures
and any sort of studio audience
and lights and cameras and
game show hosts and girls
who come along for the ride
cause in real life realize they
were all just really a bunch
of fucken phonies who never
followed through on any of their
offers and in many ways devils
only to discover paradise or
heaven is to finally at last
just be left the hell alone

"doris day dead at 99…"

34.

i am still fascinated by that recipe
for "mock apple pie" which used to
be on the side of a box of *ritz* crackers
and say "apples not required" and like
all of those things you just did not get
growing up in life had to just substitute
with other things like knowing absolutely
every statistic inside and out of each
and every ny yankee returning home
contented blood flowing with all the
muddy earth on you and skinned
knees taking warm steaming
showers knowing practically
every lyric belting bruce
springsteen made life
worth living like a piece
of that mock apple pie
apples not required

35.

in the morning i discovered they stole all
of our ships from their bottles and left us
with just bottles and simply a view of silent
suburbia ripped-off half of our framed puzzles
and took elvis's pelvis mona lisa's smile while
plucked all the feathers from our parakeet leaving
him dejected and senile muttering to himself as realized
not too ironic interestingly this is how we all kind of end up

36.

all of those outfits and the amount of time
man puts in to try and make an impression
churchill, fdr, charlie chaplin, w.c. fields
marilyn monroe, the stooges, marx brothers
and end up at best making an 'impression' or
eventually becoming caricatures of themselves

37.

while dusting off my
tchotchkes i suppose
some kind of spring
cleaning spring training
hear myself singing with
out even being aware of it
(i guess it's true about having
a predisposition for language
and all of its attributes)
johnny rotten's–
"anarchy in the uk!"

38.

i look forward to the day
when the ghosts arrive
to make me feel
more alive

39.

what's a midlife crisis for someone who's lived multiple lives?
i imagine it's alot like one of those equations where you figure
out the median and load all those numbers from top to bottom
and the one right in the middle almost from like a zen-buddhist
perspective is your answer which just feels like nothing
like watching some ole time ballgame and experiencing
phenomenon where it feels like just yesterday and know
all of the players and all of their averages and how in the
70's when they delayed the game and the camera just
stayed right on the players always knew something
crazy was happening like a brawl suddenly
breaking out in the bleachers or one of those
infamous streakers having to be wrestled down
by security right in front of that huge billboard
of *the marlboro man* sedated by the long-gone
tones of the electric organ which always just
made you feel so alone and after they hit one
out the commentators stated the name of the player
and exclaimed–"this bud's for you!" before all that
bullshit of designated drivers and drinking responsibly
and appreciating all the little things in life like knowing
every average of every ny yankee when oscar gamble
hobbles up to the plate and bends over with his infamous
stance to try and make a name which feels just like yesterday
and in a crazy-like zen-buddhist way means absolutely nothing

40.

i don't know— kind of feel during henry miller and bukowski times
(might even say joyce and gertrude stein who happened to be quite
close friends and colleagues and fond of hemingway and picasso)
couldn't get away with these o so very quasi-diverse and liberal
editors saying such shit like "no white heteros" (as if punishing
me for how i was born) i'm fucken sorry but almost seems like
a reverse form of racism and kind of close to "irish need not
apply" as if it precludes because of the color of my skin and
sexuality i must just not be diverse or sensitive enough, but
fuck them, you don't know a thing about me! if you only knew
everything i've been through and the things i've seen (and who
i have supported and stood by my whole life) and swear have
been one of the most welcoming and receptive and sympathetic
since i was a young child; of that i can promise and can't
deny! so if anything, by this selfsame dynamic and logic
and bullshit are you not the ones guilty of contradicting
and betraying your own principles and morals and ethics
while passing instant judgment, as not being diverse
and sensitive, and believe in my opinion, eventually
in the long-run, the quality and substance of
your press will suffer greatly because of it

41.

the leadership of this president
seems something like a ventriloquist
blowing air into the lungs of some dummy
desperately trying to get up his job approval rating

42.

and so amerika with your alpha-males
and misogynists and male chauvinists
and conservatives who declared in your
wheatfields and suburban lawns proudly
proclaiming out loud how you'd never
vote for hillary (you somehow strangely
made her public enemy #1 and made her
more corrupt while chanting your fight song
"lock her up!" claiming you could not trust her)
while put all your faith in someone (in some
false god you'd trust) who boasted how he
loves to grab girls by their genitalia and
shoot someone on 5th avenue and get
away with it (a murderer and rapist)
so should it really come as any
shocker that our country's now
in the shape it's in and citizens
dying off in numbers (got a roll
of paper towels for you to sob in)
by some sociopath who cares
more about his numbers (and
stock market) and approval rating
as got some good wine and a diploma
to con ya and brainwash it all down with

43.

first glimpses of a pandemic:

the town square of the village is now just
overrun by pigeons no longer jung lovers
with roses & tourists & old timers no more
running of the bulls bumpadapbumpa gondolas
the barbers & glass blowers have all closed shop
(to know it's all just some chop shop repeat "planet
of the ape" episode) no more bazooka joe with eyes
darting back & forth in the back of his head from
paranoia not sure whose side to be on anymore
no more madam butterfly shivering cold now
just fluttering in her ribbons & robes & suicide
cat-calls holed-up in the belfry of the steeple
with her romantic tragic opera moaning from
sri lanka to ole time vaudeville & delicatessens
& pickpockets & drag queens & rabbis dressed
up like perverted charlie chaplins & delicious
aroma of hot pretzels of peddlers mixed with
the stirring adrenalin of broadway boarded up
to know that orchestra warming up was always
just that protective madonna-whore sister strolling
with kid brother at dusk through the cobblestone
of brooklyn hushing him–"you could give a
headache to an aspirin!" is that whole phantom
skyline across the river in manhattan like some
stain glass window lit up by lightning now muttering
mantras at midnight–"namo-mayo-rhenge-kyo" by
the glow of a mother mary bodega candle through
the bedroom keyhole of *the times square hotel*
to know new management is still just some
ol' abuse of power absentee landlord still just
joe buck infamously tossing out that torn up
postcard like confetti zen-buddhist dreams
from the 32nd storey window of hell's kitchen
to prove he made it from the dustbowl of texas
to make a name for himself to make an honest
living as some gigolo-hustler all by his lonesome
that ole saying–"these are the times that try
men's souls" tell me something i don't know

abstract: a baseline study

during the worldwide pandemic you survive off piping
cups of *chock full-o-nuts* coffee industrial size to keep
you going and alive; a roll and pad of *hotel bar butter*
quasi-continental breakfast and those glasses rapped
up in motel plastic while the reality show president who
meets every criteria for narcissistic personality disorder
obsessive personality and borderline bordering on socio-
pathic behavior as a proud competitive and compulsive
liar continues with his lies, as this is the only way he
knows how to survive and made all his mega-millions
in the "hospitality" business still piping that propaganda
through the only 'real news' media network known to man
no longer able to follow his master plan with his campaign
rallies in the heartless heartland ignorance is bliss land of
the blind; not too long ago we used to just count down his
lies like the national debt and now not by much surprise lives

when the sun goes down over the white house
he just stands right in front of the bathroom
mirror and wipes off his clown makeup…

44.

control a:

i think if puh puh puh
i end up getting this
contemporary black
plague the last records
i want to play
are london calling,
the beatle's white album,
bach's four quartets, is that it?
and lark ascending; that balding
lounge singer still on electric piano
from the 1970's in that schmaltzy condo
down in key biscayne, florida playing over
and over again "i love you just the way you are"

45.

control b:

benjamin braddock played by the brilliant
young dustin hoffman in "the graduate"
trying with a last-ditch desperate effort
to escape and get away from his yenta
overbearing obnoxious out-of-touch
parents just sitting there in his scuba
gear at the bottom of the pool blue
brooding blowing bubbles with
his harpoon while all you hear
is just the loud amplified strained
sound mask and tank breathing aloud

46.

control c:

that scene from the movie "the hunger"
where david bowie has this bizarre
disorder where he instantly ages
out-of-control disproportionately
and while waiting in the waiting
room for his doctor to finally show
satirically has turned into a very old
man claiming something along the lines
'i warned you that this would happen!'

ex:

to me i think the one decent thing and advantage
to this pandemic in vain amerika is that people's
hair is returning back to their original color as
there's something sort of nice and natural and
distinguished about that while can't get to their
hairdresser and those little dab will do ya' jet-black
middle-aged men and middle-aged bleached blondes
at last finally going au natural sort of like when
marilyn monroe used to be a brunette going back
to simply being norma jean with a dollar and a dream

47.

control d:

what was that *twilight zone* episode again…
think it was like one of those surreal nightmares
or fantasy/dreams where he wakes up suddenly
shivering or sweating not sure which one and
turns out in fact really the opposite sensation
or phenomenon as it's the end of the world
and suppose none of that really matters at all

48.

control e:

a strange vague chart on the wall
with diagrams of slapstick stick
figures of lounge singers &
lounge singer moves & lounge
singer dance steps & lounge singer
stretches for the apocalypse & lounge
singer symptoms & lounge singer prayers
& lounge singer range of motions & lounge
singer range of (e)motions showing a lounge
singer in action in a state of flux & where
to go just in case of crisis & had enough

49.

control f:

how about whole painting
crew always just a group
of alchies or dudes just let
out of jail and at the end of
the day one of them sitting
in steaming shower nursing
a 6 pack of *pabst blue ribbon*
as isn't that i suppose
something of a form of
sublimation self-isolation
or quarantine? am i getting
that mixed up with canteen?

50.

control g:

our jesus should be a gigantic version
of that game "operation" where a whole
procession of foreboding shadows hover
over his poor scarecrow animated clown
like anatomy with those delicate tweezers
trying to remove the brain & funny bone
& moans & groans before they get that
sudden volt of electricity & be on all
day on some cable tv station till whole
damn freaken crisis is over like some
dope addict eternally nodding-out in
front of a lit-up, glowing christmas tree
in a calming, self-soothing, darkened room
& will just be like some holy-moly ceremony
of these brooding, ruminating figures moving
back & forth to just try & gingerly gracefully
remove all those internal organs from
like some psychotic, giant jesus…

51.

control h:

on the other station a nun
from the boy's group home
having developed a rope-a-dope
good and decent sense of humor
(her own form of sympathy and support
and validation) over one of those spinning
cages filled with ping pong balls almost in
a hushed tone declaring in song–"round and round
and round it goes, where it stops, nobody knows…"

52.

control i:

the boy from the back of that box of cereal
comes to life with a poster of fi-fie-fo-fum
5 food groups & table of elements behind
him simply sitting at that breakfast table
all day sounding like he's reciting the
mantras & scriptures & dead sea scrolls

53.

control j:

kids now have to look at their
laptop screens for social studies
out of home and only allowed
to tune in unless getting written
consent from a parent or guardian
wondering what they can possibly
teach them or learn about the world?

54.

control k:

for those who cannot they'll be another channel
with just a teacher's spare desk and a tape recorder
playing the constitution declaration of independence
emancipation proclamation letter from the birmingham
jail and ginsberg's howl and a camera which pans every
so often to a sill lined with dixie cups and those strange
peculiar vines growing out of them from pits inside them
and of course the token american flag draped in the corner

55.

control lmnop:

a room all filled up with tall slim
cadets decked-out in their neatly
pressed uniforms taking multiple
choice tests to fill in coveted
positions from those lifelong
experienced government
officials there for so long
let go and gone vacant done
in by the grand executioner
due to episodes of paranoia
and a threat to his power

ex:

i love what claire mcaskell said
that ex-senator from missouri
(doesn't the mississippi flow
through there?) the mentality
of that population and swath
of amerika who don't feel the
necessity to wear a mask cause
god's protecting them but still
feel the need to carry an ak-47

56.

control then q:

with too much time to kill cause time's killing me
i see on one of these grownup crackerjack surprise
channels they're selling one of those bright glowing
purple gemstone wonder woman necklaces to all those
pretty young hygienists and bank tellers whose men
all left them, and this dude with some deep southern
drawl declares–"i can't believe it's still here, but it is"
(which i sort of existentially liken to my present day
state of existence) and think in my latter years might
move down there and purchase one of those mississippi
mansions, as heard can get so much more for the buck
down in the bible belt, while maybe you might ask what
about culture but wonder what has culture ever done for me?

57.

control r:

with this crisis feels like the whole universe's stopped
like one of those good ole chinese restaurants where
the nostalgic placemats read 'year of the stray cat'
old timers passed-out at the bar from mai-tai's with
no more stories to tell charles darwin, george carlin

58.

control s:

about the only good thing with this pandemic
as no longer got any more sports in amerika
get to see those old repeats of that heated
passionate seventies rivalry between the
red sox and yankees while in fact actually
brings me right back before it all became
a business (and constantly changing teams
due to free agency) and were like family
remembering such quirky players like
mick "the quick" rivers thurman munson
who everyone loved because of his tough
pudgy coalmining demeanor and hard
work ethic and grit and determination
before he got into that tragic fatal plane
accident catfish hunter goose gossage
craig nettles who played a mean hot
corner fred "the chicken" stanley bucky
dent that sex symbol who all the girls fell
in love with; of course not so sure about
the sox cause was a diehard yankee fan
but can still remember carl "the yaz"
yastremski and carlton fisk who was
always like some consistent mythological hero
behind the plate and a threat butch hobson fred lynne

ex:

the one sobering thing about a pandemic
is you get to drink light beer a little bit earlier
(my sister who never once drank or did drugs
now drinks bourbon and think takes a shot
every evening and somehow find i have
even gained more respect for her) are able
to turn on the tv (cause sports does not exist
in america anymore and forget it all) and turn
to the 1975 world series of the big red machine
cincinatti whose team was loaded and that
expression 'feels like just yesterday' really
does feel like just yesterday and that
cognitive spiritual phenomenon of
a clear and lucid memory even though
a diehard yankee fan know everyone on
that team (might even be the greatest
along with those ole yankee teams
hearing the commentators innocently
claim how sparky anderson was such
a good ambassador for the game) pete
rose and johnny bench and tony perez
and cesar geranimo and dave conception
and ken griffey and george foster and joe
morgan all before free agency and they
stuck together like family (and don gullet
pitching in the 7th game of the world series
showing a close-up of his cute wife so young
does not quite know how to put on makeup)
thankfully taking it all from boston in fenway

59.

control t:

at least didn't take away sunday baroque
on the radio and take you right back to 1758
with bach's brilliant symphonies and concertos
which triggers when my wife actually bought me
these right before we got married living off cloisters
and would take strolls through the heather gardens
at dusk and slow dance in the window when social
work school and her mom driving us up the wall

60.

control u:

the real problem with amerika
is all the phone booth's have
been removed from the corner

everyone's on their cellphone all self-important
no place for clark kent to change into superman

61.

control v:

people make strange statements
(in how they identify with their
generation) like–"that was my war"

62.

control w:

"oi! yoi! yoi! yoi! yoi!"
translation: oi yoi yoi yoi yoi
as a breathing exercise repeat
several times oi yoi yoi yoi yoi

63.

control x:

hear wife whimpering
through the drainpipes

64.

control y:

in these days & times hear they might
consider delivering certain necessary food
items for those in need & think maybe should
also consider possibly wine & more wine & wine & wine
& wine & wine & chocolate & flowers & a rabbi & pastor
& if not into that some ol' slapstick vaudeville comedian
who tells awful corny riddles at your funeral, a stripper

65.

control z:

pretty much addicted to cable news
out of quebec, canada we get cause
way up in north country; says cirque de
soleil had to release 67% of its employees

louisville slugger factory closed down…

denouement:

and the only one left in town
will be that beatdown boy
coming from a broken house
hold tossing the newspaper
on his low-rider bicycle
domiciles designated
for perpetrators
perennials will
be out because
perennials will
always be perennials
and the dead ends
empty and vacant
cause know no different but
that's still something isn't it?

66.

the
auto
topsy
of jesus
of robin williams
of kurt cobaine
insane starving
artists reciting
their refrains
at the all-you-
can-eat dinner theater
using my ripped off
red wheelbarrow
to pick up my
scattered
bones
& brain

67.

the sign of a great film
is to be taken away to
a whole other place
in time and space
with unexpected
twists and turns
in plot dialogue
such stars were
humphrey bogart
kathryn hepburn
jimmy stewart
james dean
marlon brando
edward g. robinson

still talking about it
in the rain or not at all
brooding in the spirit of
silence on your way home

68.

the downpour falls on the parasol
of the seducing whore while all the
madmen & hustlers & drug dealers
gregarious & hysterical take shelter
on the stage where the black panthers
and hell's angels once used to rumble

you wait for it all to turn to radiant puddles
and will pick up your fried gizzard at chinese
take-out and then shuffle back to your studio
where lucky lusciano once held counsel…

you ask for very little as survival
or this thing we call our time on
earth is just waiting out the rain

69.

people talk way too much about marriage
while wondering what about divorce making
a little more of an effort and more atmospheric
bringing the ole big band back together playing
chet baker's–"if i should ever lose you" and
be just like brando in that broken ballroom
in the last scene of 'last tango' as just drop
an iou into the tip jar of the lounge singer

70.

after the murder on the midnight avenue
and the blaring spotlights have been set
up for the tv cameras who look into cars
and detour signs put up by cops just
doing their jobs dope addict parents
stagger out of *red lobster* right
around dawn on date night
as if nothing had happened
(like the remnants of some
prom or funeral procession)
upstanding citizens of the
community just going
through the motions

proof:

what happened to good ol' reliable nathan
nathan nathan nathan detroit? did he just
pick up and leave and if he did i totally
get it cause i needed to several years ago
a long time ago when i was in my early
20's with no one to fall back on all the
way out to reno— so out there didn't
even know was in the sierra-nevada's
right on the border of california; heard
there's a pretty mean mafia in montreal

proof:

those very first photos
of punch drunk san
francisco when it
was still a fishing
village on the pacifik
ocean she-cog-o before
carl sandburg & al cap
bone cohabitated just
extension of the deep
dark fertile farmland
of illinois when kansas
city & helena may very
well have even been bigger
in the cattle industry when
you still had the opportunity
to make a killing in porkbelly
soybean with the sudden holy
crash of thunder & lightning
lighting up the lobby of sleepy
silent skidrow hotels in dusty
downtown denver awaking
you out of your blind stupor
& beat down being bringing
you back down to earth & reality

71.

portland before port
land became portland
i swear i lived out there
for years all alone in my
young 20's at *the jack
london* not knowing
a living breathing
soul except for
that poor black
boy who lived
in a boxcar
studying
the bible
(in the train
yard in front
of the skyline)
and his father
was the mayor
of st. louis none
of us ever giving
up taking buses some
where around dawn into
the suburban hills to put
up cubicles for the farm o
pseudo call movers & shakers

72.

that small clean motel in reno
right up against the train tracks
of the *burlington northern* finally
left alone not knowing a living
breathing soul so broke surviving
off *kool-aid* without sugar eaves
dropping on bum's evening
conversations slipping out
6:30 in the morning 73 degrees
getting ready to wander halfway
cross the desert to try and land
some ridiculous grunt 9-5 job
working the casinos returning
home like moses broke and
brokedown woebegone refusing
to ever give up drifting back
through the desert seeing that
whole holy majestic skyline
suddenly start to light up
on fire from a mixture
of setting sun and neon

73.

just trying to make it in san francisco
like some madman's manifest destiny
real-life fugitives on-the-run having
broken parole to reunite with those
they fell in love all the way from
yonkers surviving off liquid
methadone on *greyhounds*
then spending days ripping
off ny sirloin in tenderloin
selling it half-off to the russian
hoteliers just enough to afford
a bundle of dope while lost
found lost & found nodding
out like a flickering candle at
dusk right on pharmacy corner

74.

when you just become way too lonesome…
and had had enough and know this is not the way
you were raised or brought up and hit rock bottom
make just enough to get out to napa where you chase
rich obnoxious tourists in hot-air balloons trying to tie
them down, get a part time job removing asbestos or
digging graves in graveyards, while the whole damn
procession showing up exploding–"you're not done yet?"

75.

it's the notion of time in almost any form
which does us in in the long-run and makes
us reflect and ruminate about it all; which
kills and steal one's life like a thief in the
night but likewise this selfsame dynamic
that triggers and causes us to sublimate
and create, give birth to new aesthetic
ideas and seek to redeem, while naturally
nihilistically against our own will and volition
existentially explore our own meaning and mortality

76.

all real true-blue philosophy
(existentialism & identity)
is the love/hate relationship
with fate & mortality & its
fine line between (good & bad
& right & wrong) being & reality
& all those things we have
to do & not do to keep on

77.

those always looking to make a statement
look more so impulsive, petty, and passive
aggressive; how most wars got started and
societies and cultures ended; civilization
really half an eaten boloney sandwich

78.

most riddles are simply 'short' and long-winded
looking as much for a punchline and prognosis
as they desperately are in need of an end…

79.

"is there any truth to the rumor?"
or is that one of those oxymorons
or morons just trying to start more?

80.

everything i ever said was true
dreams seem like falsehoods
you're constantly clinging
onto, or trying to prove or
me trying to be you or that
fucked-up thing of always
trying to seek approval

81.

it's an interesting perverse psychological phenomenon
in those we're constantly seeking approval are triggers
or the ones (with all their hypocrisies and contradictions)
who will never ever provide it for this selfsame reason, who
caused the original damage while all this overcompensation
is a 'desperate act' or dynamic of all the hurt and pain
inflicted and never ever having gotten closure

often we find ourselves overexplaining ourselves
to those who deserve absolutely no explanation at all

proof:

so thus those we so desperately seek approval
or to try and make an impression often appear
more like false gods, while does not that perhaps
maybe make us something like angels fallen so far?

82.

the density of matter or the measurement and
criteria of all things that don't really matter

83.

spirit— that intrinsic (other worldly) state of flux
of all things new and spontaneous that makes
one feel that spark and sense of purpose and
meaning and 'alive' in existence and reality

proof:

i got one— all of a sudden you wake up
and you got faith and your heart's open
and got nothing at all to do with anything
existential philosophical or linguistic logic

84.

whenever i hear people overuse such words
like 'spiritual' or 'spirituality' find they are not
coming close to what they are trying to describe
and always fall just short of what they desire to find

85.

on the immediacy and wild whimsy of wasting time—
to finally find out and figure out what it's all about in life

86.

how almost every culture and civilization and their (self) destruction stemmed and originated from something of a self-fulfilling prophecy

proof:

culture has a tendency more times than not
to dilute itself with way too much culture

here come the tourists who ruin it all
('to a fault') almost to the point of nausea

87.

the creation (and psychodynamic) of religion—
a macro defense-mechanism or sociological trend

88.

there's that bizarre and perverse psychological phenomenon how man is constantly searching for something 'stable' but once he gets there takes all his nihilistic and anxious energy and develops something of a neuroses of obsessive ritualistic behavior (until becomes something of a vicious cycle) to try and maintain that absurd baseline and sense of stability…

this is what we like to refer to as contemporary society

89.

what's that expression repetition's the hobgoblin—
why we're constantly searching for love and romance
or fantasy if we're lucky enough to get the opportunity

90.

looking out blinds with broken bones
make plans soon for taking off burlap
from azaleas just planted around home
getting some compost on the small
orchard planted up on hill hoping
to get some fruit this year and if
we do have this dream and fantasy
of making our own apple pies called
"mama mia/poppa pia" and selling
them right out our back porch door

proof:

from the forest door
children leap out one
by one by one by one
and somersault into
the swollen river of the
season making bird calls
completely unaware of it

complaints are made
by sexless parents...

proof:

with bouts of insomnia i want to mutely
cry out to all the gorgeous flaming perennials
growing outside the blinds of dusty mountains

91.

shattered, you toss a rock right through the window of the skyline

92.

in these desperate times that try men's souls
want to be just like one of those orthodox
rabbis in my charlie chaplin bowler and
ol' dusty tramp coat putting my dripping
schmatas up on the line, meticulously,
neat and tidy, as the subway rattles by
out to the rising sun on ocean parkway
brighton coney island to the end of the
world where i had a tiny little linoleum
room where no one knew i existed at
all after working an insane graveyard
hustling a yellow falling asleep to the
hypnotic rhythm of the distant ocean
under the influence of a 40 the morning
news and everything this life's done to me

93.

how i miss that kid who used to
sit on his roof each and every
morning in his long johns
strumming guitar i always
waved at constantly cutting
class missing-in-action
with workaholic parents
everyone looked at as
a freak but i knew as
a good kid and played
a damn good lead guitar

94.

watching ol' brilliant clip of the allman brothers
in concert beautiful hippie chicks getting down
really diggin' it dancing to the rhythm what now
these days simply looking down at their smart
phones all self-important? shit! you gotta be
fucken kidding! am i the only one who sincerely
sees the whole goddamn ridiculous tragedy of it

all— all the beauty of duane allman, dickie betts
actually i swear makes me wanna break down and
cry can't quite explain why well i can but choose not

blues #1

home movies
of mistaken
identities
be the
real
ghost
gods
miss-
under-
stood
miss-
inter-
preted
jeeze-
louise
dig the beat
take muh-
shu-ga-nah
in my coffee
the only way
i choose to
go down
remembered
not forgotten

blues #2

she left her
hightop sneakers
and long creamy legs
by my bed leaving my
head cracked open like
a pinata with all its insides
of rock hard candy spilled
out at last chill contented

blues #3

goodbye pork pie hat
she was just nice
to look at and
that's a fact
charlie mingus
cannonball adderely
get them young
in their early 20's
and prove to them
how much they
really mean to you
how you'll always
be there for them
during this world
wide pandemic
the queen
delivers
message
and that
means
something
something
similar along
the lines like
george harrison
once did like in time
all things shall pass
heard back in the day
in those ole time row
houses had so much
a sense of pride
on sunday might
even garden in tuxedos
joke to my wife being
from the bronx when
they take their tea
& crumpets and
daintily sip at it
will just bum-rush
them and say ain't

got time for this and
knock it down like a shot

blues #4

i guess all i ever needed
was to be saved on
a daily basis & to
have her sing me
an ole english
indonesian
only child
lullaby
to lull-
a-by
rock-
a-bye
moi
to sleep
at night
not even
aware
she's
singing
self-soothing
& an only child
& it only being life

blues #5

how she chooses
not just to stand
by you but lie by you
through thick & thin
threw all those early
morning melancholic
mists brooding blues
bloose bluse blews

blues #6

*WH Wants Trump To Pivot
From Virus To Economy...*
real big brother watching
there really was a reason for
warhol & jean-michel basquiat
disco dancing after vietnam...

blues #7

apparently live in such secret sophisticated
times where they got certain commercials
having to do with the topic and subject
matter of *identity theft* (narrated by an
"award-winning actor" who plays the role
of quasi-savior) which implies just in case
they try to steal your name or birthplace or
even social security number and if instantly
purchase this protection will even include
a shredder, like some sort of thematic
transactional-object which will instantly
get rid of a bad childhood or unlucky
at love or poor marriage or success
or failure in the workplace and think
if you want them they're all yours…

blues #8

o! this ol' *butch cassidy & sundance kid* existence always watching your back, while trying to just move a couple steps ahead without the so-called posse catching up to you— honey, did you remember to pack the zane grey? sunscreen?

blues #9

the discovered lost keys of the anarchist is (aint/chant) history

blues #10

wow when that angel linda rondstadt
in her sky-blue mini-skirt belted out
you're no good at the tennessee state
prison felt like just yesterday hearing
over my radio as a kid like balancing
a snowglobe on my skidrow shoulder
waiting for mistaken identity partners
to pick me up outside the interrogation
celebrating the inside job with outsiders
of this absurd reality they call existence

blues #11

looking back at one's youth & adolescence
it's them simply not getting back to you or just
saying some really mean uncalled for shit wondering
what it was you said or what you did while looking back
it was simply them with just really poor character and behavior

blues #12

besides all that infamous strength and being a stoic
about the best thing a father can teach his son is the
will to dream be a romantic and keep one's imagination

blues #13

my grandmother from flushing
queens used to do extra reading
which was the obituaries to see
if she knew anybody which seemed
like an awfully strange macabre way
or translation of that cliched expression–
"it's not what you know, but who you know"

blues #14

when you really get to know them eccentrics
are really not that eccentric at all but just
pretty damn lonesome tragic characters
constantly wrestling with their mortality
(with a 'fear of intimacy' without having
had many past substantial relationships)
often caught in some arrested stage
of development due to some profound damage
they can't (and often don't even realize) get out of

blues #15

"retailer charged with hoarding, gauging sanitizer"
and they show a picture on american online of
all these bottles all bunched together looking
like tanks ready and set up to go off into one
of those ridiculous satirical mythological battles

blues #16

yeah i guess it's true about choosing
your battles but still really sucks when
you know that they're lying (that's the
hard part of it) and becomes real draining
and trying in becoming a tired old wise man

blues #17

people apologize too simply these days
all sounding so scripted and self-effacing
(as if that was what was taught in a.a. or written
very eloquently by their agent and how to say it)
losing all of its meaning because not heartfelt or sincere
with the exact same bullshit conviction of the original betrayal

blues #18

yikes how certain people will try so hard to flatter themselves
when are so far down the cultural, hierarchal (order) ladder
and will attempt to use their arrogance and aloofness (and
indifference) to climb up it; the greatest and most obvious
mistake of "the human," ironically in itself oxymoronic

(while through this psychodynamic, whether conscious
or subconscious, try to desperately set up some form
of false prophet power-struggle and attention-seeking
when most likely were not even thinking of them, as
men of experience and wisdom can see right through)

blues #19

i always put far more into those who are loyal
as opposed to those who pretend to be royalty
while usually will discover much to your dismay
through commonplace behavioral patterns the latter
are wannabes trying way too hard to prove something
they are not, and will find in the long-run, can always
put far more trust and credence in those who can return a
simple phone call or e-mail so your life lesson for the day
don't ever be afraid, intimidated, fooled, or confused by
this selfsame role-reversal as will find the loyal ironically
are the ones pretty modest and humble and reliable
already having made it and far more successful
and don't have to act aloof or indifferent or
try so hard to prove something they are not

put your trust in the loyal over royalty...

blues #20

the truth 'lies' somewhere between what the idiots say
and don't say which is their jealous say
if you know what i'm saying

blues #21

all guys are full of shit
and guess it's just the ones
who bullshit the least that we
consider to be people of honesty

blues #22

i never needed jesus to die for me
as that saying simply made famous
by those guilty of the original crime

blues #23

can an orange in a bowl save your soul?
a bottle of seltzer? the shadows of toy
soldiers on your wall? blue-eyed girl
next door visiting son on the porch?

blues #24

can we renovate our home to make it more haunted?
build some secret set of rear stairs from the kitchen
all the way up there to some lost back hall forgotten
like a stranger we once were fond of with stray drafts
from the mad overcast season that lets in the phantoms
who whisper sweet-nothings to make us feel a little less
lonesome? maybe even sit back during that dim time of
day to take our favorite english tea with fresh bee's honey
providing their offerings from the core of the green mountains

blues #25

what weird times having
to call up *von trapp gardens*
to see if they're open this season
due to the present day plague
they did call back but just
was not in any mood
to pick up the phone
i don't know maybe
just didn't really want
an answer (is that what
they call being oppositional-
defiant or passive-aggressive?)
or a whole list of directions and
protocol for picking up perennials
(in a mask and gloves) on the scenic
side of the mountain— i don't know
sort of feels like defeats the purpose

blues #26

young angel with her pants rolled up
in rain boots exuberant with a great
attitude like some graceful horse
with sun on its shoulders hauling
buckets of water back and forth
from the river at the community
garden across the way gives
me reason to go on living

in my middle ages
it's the little things
and images like these

blues #27

when your dreams no longer
have any space or place to go
they turn to nightmares something
thought you got over a long time ago

blues #28

all my best references (and revelations) come from
long lonely solitary strolls down decadent desolate avenues
and big open majestic intellectual college quads in my nightmares

blues #29

it seems like just yesterday
that yesterday was yesterday

blues #30

a down
pour of
drizzle
falls
in the
lagoon
and
finally
at last
soaked
through
& through
by blues
in red
canoe

blues #31

they should have this phenomenon or psychological disorder
where you feel more lost when your wife throws parties for you
and wondering when your colleagues from the mental health clinic
are gonna go home, feeling so much more comfortable with your
clients who seem more grounded down-to-earth sincere and intuitive
and prefer the leftovers (like throwing a surprise party at your funeral)

blues #32

we seem to only really get and comprehend
tragedy and trauma until several decades later
when we are separated (from the incident) and
it all spiritually settles and sinks in (like fertilizer
to a flower) almost as surreal as the original violation
and betrayal but not quite exactly (as fantastic and
fragile) due to the devastating spontaneous shock
factor virtually impossible to make sense of and
all the things our mind naturally did to defend it
all that necessary compartmentalization and denial
that is why a sudden simple smell and song can
just all of a sudden break us down without even
realizing it wondering where this all came from

blues #33

when it feels like
you're constantly
being punched
in the gut
by the gods
& can only
due ye olde
rope-a-dope
& hold on
for so long
before you
just fall down
& howl some
way-out hosanna
somehow someway
somewhere between
heaven & hell between
the mountains & stars
between the deep dark
& new day materializing
on the miraculous holy horizon

blues #34

the dew from the desert
flower of the prickly cactus
starving, anxious seeing real-
life tumbleweed tumbling past
your filthy bleary-eyed bus window
at dawn, on-the-run, all looking like
some splendid slum at last far away
from home like some postmodern dystopian
neon oasis drained after they pull the plug…

blues #35

to know so much
really does depend
on a green glowing
wheelbarrow at the
end of the world like
a clown leaning up
against the flatiron
building drained in
the drizzle of dusk
how does that song
go again–"hush little
baby don't say a word"

blues #36

to know
the punch
line really
came
way
before
the rid
dull
like
where
there's
a way
there's
a will
post
humous
skeleton
& bones
of the blues

95.

the morning shows make me more blue
and not want to be around people (they
now got something called leaf gutter
protection to clean out your gutters
where very well-mannered young men
who match in their color-coordinated
green and black uniforms i suppose
to fit in with the seasons pull out
leaves and claim it's the best protection
service and #1; didn't know i needed
protection and the thing i loved to do
the most with my dad (prefer mo &
curly pulling out each other's eye
sockets with plungers) you turn to the
weather, to red river, to montgomery...

96.

the astronaut holed-up in his space capsule
is finally able to figure out if can identify
and simply readjust his posture and body
language and expressions just a slight bit
(whether it's something he's learned from
on the road or some sort of cognitive-behavioral
exercise) able to upshift from down in the dumps
to melancholia to a better overall view of life;
decides with his downtime to scribble a couple
those glossy postcards to all those girls who ended
bad and when he gets back down to earth will take
a nice warm lather and shave and plant one of those
northern red oaks; one of the few things in life he
believes won't let him down and can truly rely on

97.

the sicilians took care of us after school
at the pizza place in *the golden horseshoe*
with great big blue eyes and fine welcoming
smiles; our bikes tossed against the telephone
pole with extra garlic and *rc cola* which had that
little exotic splash of lemon as you'd thank them
and take off to the sun and peddle like mad back
home and get into trouble to reach your potential

98.

when al pacino in *the godfather* went down
to pay a surprise visit to hyman roth simply
just sitting there in his easy chair in that
ranch-style home of his in the sunshine
state eating a sandwich his wife just made
at his tv tray in front of a college football
game pretty much likening it all to the
pursuit of life, liberty, happiness and
the american way you wonder what
kind of sandwich it was and what
teams were playing, pretty much
of a repeat presentation when all
of them gathered up on top that
posh hotel rooftop in havana
looking out over all the pastel
technicolor ocean and sun and
sand celebrating his birthday sharing
a slice with the whole gang claiming
'this is the life we chose' see it
as simply differing points of view
between jean-paul sartre and camus
(between fate and free will and volition)
and of course got taken out and removed
machiavelli-style due to bouts of paranoia
(even though it turned out to be his own
coward brother fredo) even though paid
his dues and spent a majority of his adult life
working hard and not him and completely loyal

proof:

i once had this painting boss as nice as they come
a definite alcoholic but never thought much about
it, nor really cared 'cause always just drank after
we got in a full hard day's work and was one of those
real tough ole timers of courage who used to be one
of those paratroopers i think in korea, and every so
often would just come up with these really random
profound statements like the whole world depended
on it, and sounded like he really meant it, such as–
"i finally got the world beat" while being a teenager
never really knew what he meant by it and why he
kept on having the need to repeat it or say such stuff
like that, as in retrospect felt like was coming from
someone where life had most likely beat him but
now have enough experience knowing it came from
a certain place of keen hurt and pain and suffering
and insecurity often claiming he never thought he
was really smart but did run his own business and
got a lot of work due to word of mouth and used
to tell me his dream was to one day retire in a
couple of years and finally just move down to
florida and get some nice little condo and his
own boat where he could just fish forever with
out being bothered or hassled by people and never
quite sure if he ever made it down there but suppose
just having that dream made it all the worthwhile and
trust me during these present days and times and what
life does to you totally get where he was coming from

proof:

i used to have this friend i grew up with
next door and later on tried to re-explore
our friendship over *facebook* which was
cool for a little while so much entrenched
in all the bullshit politics of suburbia and
then decided to just ask him for a little piece
of advice and support in the obvious idiocy
and madness of it all and he pretty much
just summed it all up as 'it's just about who
hides it best' and knew he was right on point
but thought how pathetic; this girl i knew on
social media from vegas who was pretty nice
but one time after i guess feeling criticized
(or even ostracized) referred to herself i swear
as a 'cultural icon' and mentioned how her dad
just died yesterday and just didn't feel anything
at all and was she supposed to and thought that
was a little sad as well, and saw a sudden flash
on my tv screen of those supreme court justices
thinking what are they all for in their long flowing
black robes and photo-ops with their pure porn *polident*
smiles fine line between politics and propaganda is this
who we eventually just have to turn to and rely on when
times get rough for purposes of fairness and justice and
instantly had the spiritual revelation the only thing we
can truly rely on are the birds waking up every morn
in song outside our window at exactly 4:36 against
the pale-blue silhouetted mountains at dawn

"2 free rolls of alien tape with your order..."

proof:

some of those original westerns
show a young handsome john
wayne pointing his finger
out on the range and to that
grand expanse of manifest destiny
land on the horizon and this pretty
blonde by his side with heaps of pride
who's fallen in love with him all excited
with her heart wide open thinking about
their future while if she only knew that
amerika is all gonna just become some
perfectly pre-planned grand golf course
monochromatic condo complex divided
into plots and zones and subdivisions each
with their own shared clubhouse and pool
and list of rules eventually breaking down
in tears for no apparent reason sitting in
your sun room right around the 10th hole
during the bewitching hour when the sun goes
down homesick for the way things once were

proof:

you know sometimes i swear find myself
weeping when i think about how kerouac
spent his final remaining days down in
the sunshine state like didn't even get a
bungalow on the ocean or gulf, claiming
didn't want to live anymore so became a
drunk often found passed-out somewhere
the following morning in someone else's
backyard, as if desperately trying to make
it and take a shortcut through some strange
surreal nightmare to get to the promised land

his mom from the old country
putting his clothes up on the line...

proof:

looking back at my life i sometimes liken it to
something of a cross between clint eastwood
and some bandito but always kept it real
heart of gold and never had a mean bone
never having backed off never giving up
and kept on after they tried to threaten
(and scare me off) and betrayed me
some dwarf way up on the high wire
barely hanging on after they stole
my stilts seeing them in the pawn
shop window having to hustle to get
them back and taking shots with the
rest of the freaks of the freakshow who
wouldn't think twice to steal souls as you
stagger home from the poolhall in the darkened
cold trying to find your way back home while they'll
all forget everything they've done 'cause so lost and far
gone the following monday when return back to the job

99.

On the mythology (and life & times) of seahorses

Part I.

1

the boy with the shattered smile and hair
on fire rides his unicyle past my window

2

girls scouts with their bandoliers
on take buckshots at my home

3

women drive you up the wall
and kvetch and complain
and bicker under the last
palm tree in the world

4

if they could they'd hang one of those
pine tree car fresheners around your neck
like a locket like a noose like jesus on the cross

5

there is a reason why those old men
who worked their ass off their whole life
become dirty old men and found nodding
off on a bench on the boardwalk with the
ballroom & casino & projects behind them

6

you always hated
or just was indifferent
towards those relatives
who made those infamous
idiotic claims they have no
regrets and would do it the
exact same way all over again

and find them to be about
as sincere as one of those
compulsive lying politicians

your only regret
didn't experiment
with drugs earlier

7

that abusive family known in the neighborhood
to have the cops over every saturday evening
and then stroll to church on sunday morning
like some demented dysfunctional norman
rockwell painting like getting one of those
crackerjack surprises out the bubblegum
machine in exchange for their sins

8

time is a horseshoe
being flung in midair

9

so long
salaam
alakem

10

the ice cream truck gets
stolen right out the drive
way claims man's gotta
make an honest living
and goes on to selling
popsicles cross-country

11

plugs his hearse
into the drive-in

12

family photo are rows of butterflies
pinned by the wings like fallen angels
behind some old driftwood picture frame

13

the bowl of seahorses
has not been cleaned
out in ages…

Part II.

14

a lake of trailer park lesbians

15

flamboyant middle eastern sons who have
been banned from their parents boxcar diner

16

mischievous brothers hang from
branches of blood-orange orchards

17

morphine delivered through midnight mountains
for the final dose of a widow's last wishes

18

girls who work as all-night cashiers
at convenience stores polite and well-
mannered like angelic daughters of dead
ends making small talk with bloodshot truckers
getting their coffee and paper grateful to no longer
feel totally alienated and like eternal strangers dozing
off back down the road to unknown destinations
little less deserted down-in-the-dumps distant

19

the fishermen return home after their
two week tour for their bundle of heroin

20

the only light at dawn is in the hog farmer's home
the only one who can truly be relied on when the sound of
the sacred stirring sea comes in like a symphony through corn

21

having a place to return home and rest your bones
with a wife and son still sleeping is beyond
words and description and means the world

100.

i'm gonna come up with my own anacronym
yet wonder if in these days and times need
some kind of copyright or webpage or one
of those self-proclaimed non-prophets and
am going to call it icu and that will stand
for the very exclusive group of people of
integrity and character and unconditional
love; those who have the keen uncanny
ability to simply return a phone call and
e-mail and follow through on their word
and offer and sincerely there in mind body
spirit and soul when you sincerely need them
most in times of trouble. we will identify by
i guess kind of the few who just always been
that way and born and brought up that way
and honestly just don't know any other way

101.

to find looking back at this existence
the only one i was ever really able to
trust was a kid named robbie rifkin
remembering the exact number on
the back of his jersey (his phone
number and address and how to
take shortcuts) and feeding me
the ball on the muddy ballfield
and scoring both of us jumping
in the air as if nothing else
mattered but that moment
each one just as happy for
each other whoever it was

to know right now you're actually
older than their pretty hippie mothers

older sisters who used to flirt with you

to find in this life if get lucky
you're just like some leftover
ham on rye looking like some
beautiful broken down smile
left on a plate on the counter

Joseph Reich is a social worker who lives with his wife and fourteen-year old son in the high-up mountains of Vermont.

He has been published in a wide variety of eclectic literary journals both here and abroad, been nominated seven times for The Pushcart Prize, and has written over twenty books of poetry and cultural studies.

He wholeheartedly agrees with Voltaire and Neil Young that man needs a maid, and still trying to make his way through *Finnegan's Wake*.

www.ingramcontent.com/pod-product-compliance
Lightning Source LLC
Chambersburg PA
CBHW030852170426
43193CB00009BA/586